THE WIND OF FIRE

REVIVAL CONTINUES

Due to the overwhelming response of thousands to the present awakening in the United Kingdom, through the commitment to God's guidance of the Rev. Melvin Banks, his family and their team, he personally or one of his family would be happy to make themselves available to visit your town, city, suburb, church or fellowship, in order to share these amazing stories and testimonies. Please contact the address given below.

Also, if you would like further copies of this book, or other books by Melvin Banks – *Faith Unlimited*, *Is Anything Too Hard for God?*, *The Greatest Miracle*, *Radiant Living*, *Power for Living*, *Healing Secrets* – you can get them either through your local Bible bookshop or by writing to the Crusade office.

The Rev. Melvin Banks welcomes letters, invitations, prayer requests for you or your loved ones.

Also available are videos, tapes and free literature. For the latest news of the Revival send a stamped addressed envelope to:

The Rev. Melvin Banks
International Crusade Office
44 Monks Way
Chippenham
Wiltshire
SN15 3TT
England

Melvin Banks has written a sequel, with fresh and up-to-date information on the Revival, in a book coming out from HarperCollins in 1993, entitled *The Fire Burns On*. Order it early!

THE WIND OF FIRE

Signs of Revival Today

MELVIN BANKS
with Simon Fox

MarshallPickering
An Imprint of HarperCollins*Publishers*

Marshall Pickering is an imprint of
HarperCollins*Religious*
Part of HarperCollins*Publishers*
77–85 Fulham Palace Road, London W6 8JB

First published in Great Britain
in 1992 by Marshall Pickering

1 3 5 7 9 10 8 6 4 2

A catalogue record for this book is
available from the British Library

ISBN 0 551 02504 2

Typeset by Medcalf Type Ltd, Bicester, Oxon
Printed and bound in Great Britain by
HarperCollinsManufacturing Glasgow

CONTENTS

CHAPTER 1

The Revival Has Begun!

> . . . men of Issachar, who understood the times and knew what Israel should do . . .
>
> *(1 Chronicles 12:32)*

God is coming down upon Britain today in great power. Mighty miracles are being reported from all quarters. The remnant are seeking their God, and the Almighty has seen fit to hear them. Revival is bursting forth. Christians are dedicating themselves to the pursuit of holiness and submitting to the lordship of Christ. In places faith is reaching fever pitch. The Church has been asleep for the past forty years, but parts of it have now begun to wage intensive warfare against the enemy.

There is no doubt that God has begun something special in the United Kingdom. We are no longer looking, waiting and hoping for revival, for *it has begun*. It has broken out in these islands! In many different places truly remarkable things are happening. This revival could even outshine and overshadow the revivals which took place in the Hebrides, Wales and Ulster during the past century. The love and power of Jesus is coming in waves, not only to Christians but also to countless unsaved people. The harvest on the local level has never been greater in living memory.

The time is ripe for revival

Britain is now ripe for revival; the conditions are right. Millions are finding that there is much about life which disappoints them. They try to drug themselves with materialism, sex and pleasure of all kinds, hoping that these things will kill the pain they feel and fill their emptiness. Millions of our fellow countrymen are going straight to hell in their Volvos and Rovers and BMWs. During the last decade Britain has seen a good deal of prosperity. As I visit town after town in the course of my work I see new housing estates springing up on sites that were once just farmland. My work takes me to many different parts of the country, but wherever I am, on Sundays I always see the same sight – people washing and polishing their cars. This is their Sunday morning religious ritual: they bow down and worship their shiny metal gods. But those gods in their driveways cannot answer prayers or heal sick minds and bodies or change lives . . .

Once there was a certain British product which bore the reassuring trademark, "I never disappoint". But countless British people are disappointed about life. This disappointment touches all ages – even the young. They may study hard at college or university, only to find at the end of it all that they either have no job to go to or else have to enter the commuter ratrace, seemingly trapped for life.

Years ago there was a pop song which went:

I woke up today, I was crying,
lost in a lost world.
So many people are dying,

lost in a lost world.
Oh, can you feel the world pining,
pining for someone who really cares?

So many people are lost, living in a tunnel of darkness. They don't know who they are, why they are here or where they are going. They have lost their way, their hope, their identity in life. The famous German philosopher Schleiermacher was once sitting on a park bench looking up at the stars, quietly wondering about the purpose of life. A policeman came by and shone his lamp in his face, asking, "Who are you?" The great thinker replied, "I don't know. I wish I knew who I was." Many British people today are in the same spiritual state as he was. Yes, the time is ripe for revival. People are ready to hear the Gospel, and God wants a Church ready to preach it.

Holy, committed people

A small minority in the Church are already fully caught up in the revival, as this book will show. They are holy, committed people with hearts consumed by God's Spirit. In His power they are turning the tables on the enemy. God is rallying the remnant – people who understand the times and know their God, who want to illuminate and rescue this dark world. These people are not a clique of dull, repetitious know-it-alls who fail to produce the fruit of the Spirit. Christians like that are being bypassed. Instead God is using loving, worshipping, humble, compassionate, Christ-centred, soul-winning disciples – they are on His heart and under His mighty reviving hand. He is saying, "Let the dead bury their own dead, but you go and proclaim the kingdom of God" (Luke 9:60).

It is not correct heads but consecrated hearts that He is touching. He is not using Christians who merely know the facts; He is using those who have been set on fire by those facts. God is showing us that one man with the fire of God in his heart is worth a library full of arguments.

Across the land many Christians are saying, "Whatever it costs me, I want to do what God wants me to do!" A new type of firebrand is appearing – the Christian who has an increasingly holy fellowship with God. The Word of God is coming alive in countless hearts, and the result is action, conviction, signs, wonders, miracles, holiness, power, a flood of converts, expansion, all-night praying, immense church planting, compassionate ministries and changed lives. Once many Christians, because they were afraid of offending people, were not being effective, but now their eyes are opening and they are returning to their first love. They are beginning to see that they are called to illuminate the world – indeed, that they are "the light of the world" (Matthew 5:14). Now many believers, instead of crawling around in the dark, are flooding the land with light – and that light has no communion with darkness.

Honesty, love and brotherhood are returning to a few in the Church. There is a new emphasis on renouncing competition and pointless duplication, on repenting of selfishness, suspicion, slander, narrow ambition and empire-building. Forgiveness, conviction and the fear of God are falling on us.

Thank God that things are changing. Instead of pathetic ministries God is giving us prophetic ministries.

The Obadiahs who compromized by going out to look for grass with the Ahabs instead of praying for rain with the Elijahs (1 Kings 18) are being left behind. A new breed of leaders is arising. These are people who have no interest in prestige, position and denominational favours and instead seek the anointing of God.

Some Christians are finding fault with what is happening now – they cannot believe that this is it, that this is the revival which they have longed and waited for. They have talked, prayed, lectured and written about revival, but they despise the Micahs who are now announcing that revival has come. Such Christians may criticize as much as they wish, but their words will not stop the revival.

An "epidemic" of revival

As we get closer to God and listen to Him and obey Him, an ever-increasing number of people are turning to Christ; "those who have not heard will understand" (Romans 15:21) – we are seeing it happen before our very eyes. As we hear His voice and go out into the world in His name, "the Sovereign Lord will make righteousness and praise spring up before all nations" (Isaiah 61:11).

God is at work in an awesome way today. Heaven is on our side. God is sweeping through the spiritually starving multitudes and His kiss of forgiveness is touching them. An "epidemic" of revival has broken out, bringing great defeat to the evil one and great glory to the Living God. The power of the Lord is being reinstated; God is miraculously raising up the casualties of the twentieth century.

In the days of Jonah the king of Nineveh commanded his people, "Let everyone call urgently on God. Let them give up their evil ways and their violence" (Jonah 3:8). This was the result: "When God saw what they did and how they turned from their evil ways, he had compassion and did not bring upon them the destruction he had threatened" (verse 10). Today we too are witnessing God's compassion and forgiveness. The heart of this nation is being touched by His love as never before. We are seeing the mystical, majestic, mighty God at work amongst us.

We are living in an extraordinary period in the history of this country, so this is not the time to live ordinary lives! God is calling us to be extraordinary people. Never in living memory have we seen in this land the like of the revival power which God is sending now. *Let us seize it, let us press through in it, let us spearhead it into every corner of the nation!*

God is sovereign; He is in charge, He is all-powerful, He is giving us the victory, He has granted us this revival power, this favour, this grace, this joy, this harvest – *but he is working through us!* The revival is our responsibility – let us not fail to grasp with both hands what God is giving us today!

In this book you will read of the many thousands of lives which are being changed by the power of God today, of the astounding miraculous signs which are being witnessed, of the unparallelled revival growth which is taking place, of the fresh reviving power of the Holy Spirit which is being clearly manifested. You will read of amazing awakenings among the homeless, ethnic groups such as the Gypsies and subcultures such as the "biker" gangs; you will read of a new visitation of God among working-class people and in rural and suburban areas which hitherto have been spiritually cold and hard. You will read about the unpleasant side of revival – the opposition and resistance which it is encountering. And you will read about some of the central characteristics of the revival and those involved in it, such as an absorbing love of prayer, extreme sacrifices of time, money and patience, a fervent grasping of and teaching of biblical truth, and a passionate zeal in serving Jesus. In this book I write about the revival as I have seen it and experienced it in my ministry. Of course, other preachers and evangelists could also tell some fascinating stories about their own involvement in the present move of God in Britain.

The newspapers – national and local – are starting to feature the revival at length. The *Sunday Times Magazine* recently ran a feature by Ian Cotton on the current awakening, entitled "Bless my soul – the rise of the New Christians":

> Miracles . . . so routine in the Bible, so remote from the traditional church . . . are a feature of their services. On offer is the complete supernatural agenda . . . beyond worship, beyond morality, beyond doctrine . . . it is a manifestation of a world-wide, massive revival of Christianity underway . . . one of the great untold stories of our time, but not the Christianity which most of us know . . . the new Christians are spontaneous, passionate, noisy, obsessed with God's miracle-working immediacy, yet highly conservative in doctrine. The attraction is plain: the world becomes more relativist each year . . . yet a rock remains – the moral absolutes. Everywhere the story is the same: conventional,

> formalistic Christianity continues to decline; but inspirational, rollercoaster Christianity is in prodigious advance . . . we are in the midst of the grandest upsurge in church history, a veritable "third wave", introducing a new phase and intensity of Christian experience . . . the floodtide is truly lapping on our shores. The Bishop of Bradwell (Essex) called it "a great hope for the future", but whatever your view is of the new Christians, singalong or shudder, this much seems beyond doubt: the future is theirs.

That's what this book is about – the new revival, the New Christians in Britain today. *The future is theirs!*

CHAPTER 2

A British Revival!

This is the real thing!

(said recently by one of the last surviving converts of the 1904 Welsh Revival)

They moved out of the realm of the common and the natural into the sphere of the supernatural . . . and that is Revival.

(Duncan Campbell)

I do not always give details of places, since some pastors might not be able to cope with masses of post, but anyone wishing to should write to our office (see p. 2). Recently I stood before a large gathering of people in this fishing town in the north of Scotland. This was just one of the thousands of evangelistic meetings which I had led over the past thirty years; little did I know that the events of that evening were to be very much out of the ordinary!

All of that day I had been praying, concerned about what needed to be done to bring the nation back to God. I had heard on the radio that day that the national crime and suicide rates were rising, and that even the north of Scotland, traditionally a religious part of the country, was becoming more materialistic. I had read in a newspaper that a recent survey in Northern Ireland had revealed that since the troubles there had begun twenty years ago the province had become more secular; many people there were losing their faith.

God had graciously used me over the past thirty years to bring salvation and healing to many people. That was a cause for thanksgiving and satisfaction, but I somehow wanted more than I had so far seen. I knelt in prayer that afternoon, with the sound of the seagulls' song in my ears and the fresh, salty tang of the sea air in my nostrils. And as I prayed in my little room I suddenly felt that the Lord was very close to me and that He was giving me a strong anointing and an assurance that He was going to do something which I had as yet not seen. I was lost in wonder, enveloped in His love and power; it was as if His light lit up the room. I praised Him with my whole being. *God was going to do someting more!* The word *purity* kept passing through my mind: God was saying, "I want you to be pure." That afternoon He convicted me of my sins and bathed me in His forgiveness and cleansing power. I submitted to this and thanked Him and adored Him.

After all that I wondered what it might be that the Lord was going to do. Perhaps there would now be even more converts at my campaigns than there had been in the past. I looked forward to seeing God do something amazing when I moved on to my next mission, which was south of the Border.

But the Lord had other plans; He was going to do this new work there in that little Scottish town. I was preaching my sermon that night, presenting my usual message about the crucified Saviour. I looked at the crowd of people who had listened. The Highlanders are lovely folk, but they tend to be rather sober and cautious; they don't like anything out of the ordinary. The people in the church that evening had listened to me with interest, but they had not been visibly moved.

But suddenly my legs gave way beneath me, and in a moment I was lying flat on my face on the platform! I felt the presence of God – an overwhelming, glowing, holy elation. Then I began to come to, and I felt embarassed. Even though God's Spirit was at work upon me powerfully at that moment, I was still able to think a few rather unspiritual thoughts. "Here I am," I thought, "a respectable Pentecostal minister – behaving like this!"

I had always recoiled from hyper-emotionalism. Falling down like this was almost a taboo with me. Thousands of people had been healed in my meetings, but generally they had not fallen about, they had not screamed. I never liked that sort of thing. But there I was that night, among some of the most unemotional, reserved people in the British Isles – lying flat on my face in the middle of my sermon!

I thought of the very free and happy Mount Zion Church in Norwich, where I had preached annually for years. It was a church renowned for its very lively meetings. "Now there," I thought, "this sort of thing would be acceptable – but not here! One thing is for sure – I'll never be asked to come and preach here again!"

Then I lifted myself up slightly and saw that the church's two pastors, who had been sitting on either side of me, were also lying flat on their faces! "Oh well, that's not so bad, then," I thought; "it's not just me – God is dealing with them too."

Then, still unable to get up, I strained to see what effect the weird antics of the three preachers had had upon the congregation. To my dismay I found that I couldn't see anyone! Where were they? Had they all gone home in disgust or fear? "Of course, they don't know that we're not doing this deliberately, that we're helpless in God's hands," I mused. "So we have lost them all. But why has God gone and lost the whole congregation? What can that possibly achieve?"

Then I strained a bit more and was able to see a bit better, and found to my amazement that I hadn't been able to see the congregation for the simple reason that they too were all flat on their faces – on the floor in between the rows of seats, in the aisles, everywhere and anywhere. There wasn't a single person standing or sitting! An awed, sweet silence pervaded the whole building. Soon I could hear an occasional sob, or someone praying, "Forgive me, Lord!" or crying, "I've found God at last!" or saying with a deep sigh, "Thank you, Lord!"

Revival had come to that church, to that town! Hours later – well past midnight – we got quietly to our feet. It was a night to remember . . .

Some days later I was deep in prayer about my future ministry, and the Lord said to me, "I want to give you more."

I was taken aback by that, and foolishly I tried to tell the Lord all that I had already achieved for Him in my ministry. The blind had received their sight, the paralyzed had been healed, the deaf had had their hearing restored, drug addicts had been released from their bondage, broken homes had been brought back together again. Once a dead man had even been raised up! There had been thousands of converts, nearly fifty churches had been planted across Britain, there had been powerful missions in Europe, Asia and Africa. I told the Lord all this, as if He didn't know far more about it than I did, and as if it had been my work rather than His. I felt that I had done enough; I wasn't sure that I wanted the Lord to give me any more!

I said, "I'm booked nearly a year ahead, I'm preaching in up to ten countries each year, I'm in planes more often than I'm in cars. Souls are getting saved every day, my books are selling in tens of thousands, spreading the message. Isn't that enough? What more do you want?"

The Lord simply replied, "I want to give you a revival."

"But Lord, I've been involved in revivals in Third World countries. I know Dr Yonggi Cho in Korea well. I've been in the great visitation in Africa . . ."

The Lord said, "I want to give you a revival *in Britain*."

From that time onwards my evangelistic ministry was on a new level of power and effectiveness. After the mission in Scotland I went to County Durham to lead a campaign. God blessed it so powerfully that the police had to be called out to control the traffic, since so many people were trying to get to the meetings. About 1,000 people passed through the enquiry rooms during the mission. Then I moved on to a large town in Lancashire. The campaign was based at the Assembly of God church there, which had only about 40 members. It was an old church, and so it had some of the traditions which can be a hindrance to the pouring out of God's "new wine". However, over the five weeks of the campaign 2,100 people responded to my invitation to give their lives to Christ. The local papers interviewed me and devoted whole pages to reports of the miraculous healings which were taking place. There was no sophisticated evangelistic strategy or organization behind this – just a small group of Christians praying, fasting and working with great faith, and so seeing a massive move of God amongst thousands of the non-churchgoers of this huge working-class district. Today there are fifteen full-time workers and ministers in that church. About twenty other people have gone out from it as pastors and missionaries. About 1,000 people now attend its sevices every week, which are held in a large disused cinema in the centre of town.

I have preached the Gospel in many different parts of the world, and the response to the message has often been astonishing. People have come forward to give their lives to Christ in their hundreds and thousands; I have seen innumerable people healed from diseases by the power of God. I have mentioned much of this in my other books. But what I want to emphasize in this book is that *we are now seeing similar things happening in this country* on an unprecedented scale. Once it was thought that revival of that sort was only for far-away countries in the Third World, and that as far as revival was concerned we in Britain had had our day. But a revival of a truly biblical type is now taking place in our land. Miracles are happening, mountains are being moved and hitherto unbelieving pagans are being converted in large numbers. Older churches are being rejuvenated and new ones are springing up all over the place. *True revival has come to Britain!*

Unorganized – suddenly – unpremeditated!

CHAPTER 3

A Vision of Revival

> The time of the singing of the birds is come and the voice of the turtledove is heard in the land.
>
> (*Song of Solomon 2:12* – Amplified Bible)

What is revival? Recently I asked some Christians to define it, and I received varied answers. I was told that revival was "many people finding Christ" or "the Holy Spirit being real amongst His people" or "miraculous gifts being displayed". I have seen all of these things happening across Britain over the past thirty years, but that was not revival!

The Hebrew word *hecheyah* is used some forty times in the Old Testament and means "recover" or "restore to life". It is used of the great revivals which happened in the times of Nehemiah and Ezra. Psalm 85:6 says, "Will you not revive us again, that your people may rejoice in you?" In Habakkuk 3 we have the prophet's famous prayer for revival: "O Lord, revive thy work in the midst of the years" (verse 2, AV). In the New Testament the Greek word *amazopureo* is used. For example, Paul advises Timothy to revive or "fan into flame the gift of God, which is in you" (2 Timothy 1:6).

Tozer defines revival as "that which changes the moral climate of a community"; Havner calls it "the saints getting back to normal"; Arthur Wallis says it is "such a manifestation and working of God, that human personalities are overshadowed, man is in the background, and God is taking the field". Revival is more than successful evangelism: in evangelism we are working for God, but in revival God is working on behalf of us. In revival the righteousness and power of God are made manifest in events beyond human control, such as deliverances from demons, miracles and wonderful conversions.

Revival is not a cultural or social phenomenon, but a visitation of God. Revival is more than big meetings. It is more than religious excitement. It is more than the saints being filled with the Holy Spirit. It is more than large numbers of people being converted. One may have any of these things without revival, and yet revival includes them all. There is a wealth of difference between evangelistic missions and campaigns at their best and genuine revival. In the former man takes the initiative, with the prompting of the Spirit; in the latter the initiative is God's. In the former the organization is human; in the latter it is divine. Missions may be part of the continuous programme of evangelism which is the task of the Church, but revival is a special phenomenon which happens at special times. It may, of course, break out during a mission; when it does, certain features will appear which are peculiar to revival, while certain features which are characteristic of missions will disappear. When revival happens and tarries, the normal evangelism of the Church must continue. However, let us keep the distinction between revival and mission clear.

Peter said of the outpouring of the Holy Spirit at Pentecost, "this is what was spoken by the prophet Joel: 'In the last days, God says, I will pour out my Spirit on all people'" (Acts 2:16-17). Revival is essentially a manifestation of God. It has the stamp of Deity upon it, which even the unregenerate and the uninitiated are quick to recognize. Revival must of necessity make an impact upon the community in which it happens. Recently I witnessed such a visitation of God in a densely crowded hall in the Bristol docks. I could only stand in awe-struck silence as wave after wave of divine power swept through the place. Mere minutes after the arrival of this heaven-sent breath, men and women were on their faces in emotional, mental and spiritual distress.

Colin Whittacker has said, "Revival is God by His Spirit bringing back to full and vigorous health His 'half-dead' people." If we are to have revival, we must be prepared for our dead churches and dull ministries to be drastically disturbed by an inflow of divine life. Also, we must be prepared to accept that that divine life may operate in unexpected ways. Duncan Campbell wrote, "Those who seek God for revival must be prepared for God to work in His own way and not according to their programme." P. Jennes says revivals are "supernatural demonstrations of God's power . . . when will we spend more time in seeking to know what is his way than we do in devising human plans and methods? . . . we need revival, the Church needs revival, the world – hungry, restless, sin-cursed, dying – needs a revival. God wants us to have it . . . let us meet divine conditions and . . . expect him to answer by fire."

Vision must come before revival

Every great revival starts with a vision. Vision leads to renewal and renewal, if followed through, leads to revival. The Bible offers many examples of this process. Josiah had a vision – a glimpse of what God required. Isaiah had a vision of God's glory. Ezra's and Nehemiah's vision was the rebuilding of Jerusalem, and this led to a revival in the life of the Jewish people.

In this country today the vision which we need is being rekindled by God in three ways. First, God is giving people a vision of Himself. Isaiah had a vision of the holiness and magnificence of God: "I saw the Lord seated on a throne, high and exalted"; he saw seraphs who were calling to one another, "Holy, holy, holy is the Lord Almighty; the whole earth is full of his glory" (Isaiah 6:1, 3). God is holy, so His people must be holy too; their motives for wanting revival must be right. Holiness and revival go together.

Let's pause for a moment and ask ourselves why we want revival. How much does our own gain figure in our thinking about it and our praying for it? R. A. Torrey wrote in this connection: "Many prayers for revival are purely selfish. The churches desire revivals in order that the church may have a position of more power and influence in the community, in order that the church treasury may be filled, in order that a good report may be made by the presbytery or conference or association. For such low purposes God cannot answer."

If we are to have revival, we must first have clean hands and pure hearts. Isaiah wrote, "Come out . . . and be pure, you who carry the vessels of the Lord" (52:11). We need to bring before God all those things that grieve Him, and we need to be cleansed by Him: "Cleanse me with hyssop, and I shall be clean; wash me, and I shall be whiter than snow" (Psalm 51:7). As Augustus Toplady wrote:

Let the water and the blood
From thy riven side which flowed,
Be of sin the double cure,
Cleanse me from its guilt and power.

Secondly, God is giving us a vision of the need around us. Jesus saw the need, and was moved with compassion by it. Like so many believers today, His disciples wanted to put off the task of evangelism, but He said to them, "Do you not say, 'Four months more and then the harvest'? I tell you, open your eyes and look at the fields! They are ripe for harvest" (John 4:35). The great William Booth, founder of the Salvation Army, declared that if he had his way he would not send his trainee officers to a Bible college, but would instead send them to hell for an hour; then "they would come out on fire for lost souls".

Thirdly, God is giving us a vision of the glorious blessing which we can have if we are willing to be channels through which it can flow. God wants us to be "one-hundred-percenters". The Bible and Church history are full of the stories of committed people through whom God was able to work powerfully. Gideon, even though he had only 300 men, defeated a vast army of enemies. We can think of plenty of other channels of God's blessing, such as Abraham, Isaac and Jacob; Peter, Paul, John and James; Augustine, Luther and Calvin; Wesley and Whitfield; Billy Bray and W. P. Nicholson; Smith Wigglesworth, Evan Roberts, Duncan Campbell and Douglas Scott; D. L. Moody, Percy Brewster and David Wilkinson; Yonggi Cho, Jackie Pullinger and Reinhardt Bonnke. The words on the grave of a great missionary in the South Sea Islands read, "When he came there was no light; when he died there was no darkness." He had been a channel for God's blessing.

The same God who worked through the celebrated saints of the past is today working through many Christians in many parts of this country. God is giving us a vision of the impossible being achieved everywhere through ordinary Christians. They are dreaming dreams, seeing visions, seizing territory from Satan, achieving goals for God and turning the tables on the enemy. Throw yourself upon the Lord and ask Him for a vision of a mighty revival in the big cities, the towns and the villages. Capture His vision of a sparkling, purified Church, of a vital, militant, burning, radiant, holy, active, fruitful, miraculous, faithful, loving people who will set Britain on fire from its tip to its toe.

With Christ "the saints of the Most High will receive the kingdom and will possess it for ever – yes, for ever and ever" (Daniel 7:18). *We are building the Kingdom!* Many Christians are finding their place in it, discovering the part which they must play and identifying their gift or talent or niche.

During the early stages of the building of Liverpool Cathedral an American visitor approached a workman and asked him what he was doing. The man replied, "I'm mixing mortar." The visitor asked a second man, "And what are you doing?" He replied abruptly, "Carrying bricks!" The American then went over to a third man, a bricklayer, and asked him the same question. He drew himself up to his full height and answered proudly, "I am building a cathedral!" That man had vision. We need to be like him: we need to remember that no matter how humble our work for God may seem to be, it is a part of the building of His Kingdom.

Revival starts with you and I

In the past there were never any short cuts to revival, and there are none now. *The only way to revival is prayer.* And that prayer must begin with you and I. Allow the Holy Spirit to set your life alight with the match of praying faith.

Let the fire spread through your church, and then through your neighbourhood, your town and even your nation. Let the fire start now. If not now, when? If not you, who? If not here, where?

Someone once asked the celebrated evangelist Gypsy Smith how they could begin a revival. He replied, "Draw a circle and stand in the middle and ask God to revive everything inside that circle!"

Revival starts with individuals and affects individuals. During the Welsh Revival some people came to Cardiff, looking for the move of God which had set recently that city alight. In the city centre at the rush hour, they saw a policeman on traffic duty in the middle of the road. They asked him where the revival was. "In here," he replied, pointing to his heart and smiling. He had been saved at one of the revival meetings.

God is looking for men and women who will be His emergency task force to combat the forces of the devil. The Holy Spirit wants volunteers who will be at full alert whenever there is a crisis. I have volunteered; have you?

We are at a crucial point in the history of the Church. The enemy knows that the hour is late and is poised to attack every Christian individual, family, church and organization. But we must stand our ground and fight the good fight – we must be the salt of the earth. Will we fulfil this God-given responsibility, or will we ignore the signs of the times?

The revival is under way – it is a real, biblical, localized, British revival! A Holy Ghost earthquake has begun. The cracks are appearing in Satan's kingdom as God's Kingdom advances. Pray for it, hold on to it tightly, spread the Good News! Don't doubt and miss out on what God is doing in this land today!

CHAPTER 4

Entering a New World

> They shall declare the work of God, and shall wisely consider . . . His doing(s).
>
> *(Psalm 64:7-9)*

A while ago my wife and I went window-shopping at Harrods in London. Above the main entrance was a slogan which had been there for a hundred and twenty years: "You are entering into a new world". Those words could have been written about the present revival. Lewis Carrol's *Alice Through the Looking Glass* is a wonderful illustration of this. Alice walks up to the mirror, passes through it and enters a new world on the other side. Everything is different there – back to front, new and fresh. The same is true of the Kingdom of God which we are tasting in this revival. It is changing things radically and rapidly. God is turning things upside down! Our churches may have been dull and weak, but now they are alive, vibrant, exciting and growing, having been transformed by the power of the Spirit. It's getting more wonderful by the hour. No more boring, irrelevant, traditional, legalistic mumbo-jumbo! Instead the Church is becoming a people moving in the Holy Spirit, bringing God's Gospel message and power to this country.

The revival has brought about a major change in the whole character of evangelism. It used to be hard work, the results of which were often minimal. But now it is much easier to lead people to Jesus. Now when a church plans a mission it is not unusual for hundreds of non-churchpeople to phone, asking for help and prayer. They don't even wait for the mission to start!

In the revival meetings we feel an unusual atmosphere. It seems to be tingling with the Divine, impregnated with the Almighty. There is a wonderful aura of sacredness, a sense of the richness of God – you can feel that the Saviour is everywhere around you! People are often touched by the Spirit of God as they enter a meeting or as they sit in their seats. They are convicted of their sins and start to weep. Often folk fall on their knees in the pews, and many of them find Christ before the preaching even begins. Countless times people have been healed during the sermon or the worship, without receiving the laying on of hands.

A while ago I met one of the converts of the Welsh Revival of 1904. She was a thin, pale elderly lady, and yet her mind was alert and her eyes shone as she told me about her experiences during that amazing revival. Evan Roberts' meetings used to go on all night until six in the morning, when it was time for the men to go to work down the pits! There were always long queues of people waiting to get into the chapels. There were cries for mercy, earnest prayer and much weeping. A divine light seemed to shine from the faces of Roberts and the other preachers.

When I met this lady I was holding meetings in South Wales, the heartland of the old Revival. She told me that she was seeing the whole thing being repeated. "It was just like this," she said. "The healing part of it was not known so much then, but the conversions were just like the ones we're seeing now. And the feeling you get in the meetings now is like it used to be. It was wonderful back then – but this is wonderful too – this is real! Oh, to think that I should have lived to see it all again!"

Today we are seeing the fulfilment of this prophecy: "see if I will not throw open the floodgates of heaven and pour out so much blessing that you will not have enough room for it" (Malachi 3:10). In the present revival we are indeed seeing abundant blessing. We are experiencing the threefold blessing of the Gospel: salvation from the power of sin, healing from disease and deliverance from the dominion of demons.

In recent years among various groups of praying, believing people in different parts of the country there grew up a deepening belief that the time had come when God was going to favour us with a rich outpouring of His Spirit. Prayer was intensified, faith was encouraged, expectation advanced and many came to believe that something would happen. In numerous places people received a vision from God. They had no contact with eachother at that time and did not know that others were receiving the same vision. But gradually it became clear that God was saying the same thing to many people in different parts of the country.

I was one of those who received that vision. Normally I am rather cautious about such things, but I had no doubt that this was from God. He gave me a vivid picture of a great waterfall. I was drowning in it, and it was flowing over God's people, going over their heads. The flood continued until it covered all the land and all the people around us. It was a powerful, joyous, God-glorifying vision! Some time later I described this vision to a Lancashire pastor with whom I was crusading. By the time I had got about half way through it he had turned pale, and then he finished it for me! He had seen exactly what I had seen – his description of the vision was word for word the same as mine! During that month-long crusade we saw something of the fulfilment of the vision, for 2,000 people were converted. Now the Assemblies of God in that town have 1,000 attenders and meet in a huge cinema.

There has been a huge breakthrough in Coventry and the Midlands amongst the immigrant community. In 1991 in one week I prayed for two thousand, mostly Sikh, Hindu or Muslim. The power of Christ became the talk of the hindustani community. In one Black Country town, the popular pub virtually emptied nightly, the drinkers cheering as once-crippled people walked home from revival meetings in scores. They stood in the streets outside the meeting place to see the miracles of God.

We are now seeing people show an interest in God who would once never have dared enter a Christian church. This is God's new day. We are crossing Jordan and pulling down the strongholds of Jericho. In a Buddhist area of Bristol, St Werburgh, four lonely saints, in an area where almost every church was closed down, prayed, holding fourteen prayer meetings in a week. A new day dawned, miracles happened and many were saved. The Buddhists who tried to hinder the meetings by chanting ran off when they saw empty wheelchairs pushed home. A new church has been born.

CHAPTER 5

Mighty Miraculous Manifestations

I will . . . multiply my miraculous signs and wonders . . .

(Exodus 7:3)

During His earthly ministry many sick and crippled people were brought to Jesus' feet, and He raised them up with a touch or a word. The same thing is happening in the new wave of God's power which is now sweeping across this land – Jesus is still healing people! Here are just a few of the many stories I could tell of God's mighty miraculous manifestations in the present revival.

An entire congregation is converted

On a number of occasions I have preached at the Aston Christian Centre near the heart of the city of Birmingham. This is the sort of working-class inner-city area which is difficult to evangelize. Here there is a large ethnic non-Christian population who in the past have shown no interest in the Gospel. There are also serious social problems such as unemployment, street crime and vandalism. As a result people tend to lock and bolt their doors at night and seldom venture out, and so it is hard to get them to come to Christian meetings. So it was a sure sign of the power of God working in the area when the evangelistic campaign which I led there five years ago met with a huge response. People flocked to the meetings, and many were converted and touched by God's healing power. ITV Central broadcast news stories about it all, interviewing the people who had been healed. Since then the church has grown so much that it now holds its Sunday meetings in a large auditorium. No other local event can draw crowds like that. God has revived this tough, spiritually barren inner-city area in a remarkable way.

Recently I led another campaign at the Aston Christian Centre. Bill Hopley, the minister, had invited a preacher from Jamaica to take part in the campaign, and on the first night he and I were preaching simultaneously in different halls. There are not many churches in the UK which are able to run two big events on the same night! But they expected large numbers of people to attend, and they were not disappointed – both halls were full.

My meeting the following afternoon was crowded to the doors well before it was due to start. The audience was very mixed – black, white, Indian, Pakistani, Chinese. All the religious groups from the area were represented – Roman Catholic nuns, Anglicans, Free Church people, Sikhs, Moslems, Hindus and Taoists.

A pain-riddled, paralyzed man was brought to the meeting in an ambulance car. The three nurses who had come with him laid him on a bed in one of the aisles. They propped him up so that he could see what was going on. Many of the people in the crowd must have thought, "What on earth can be done for that poor man? Can God heal him?"

Yet more people arrived, squeezing into every corner and sitting in the aisles. The windows had to be opened to prevent the air from getting stale – there were so many people breathing it! Hymns were sung as the last people came in, and then the service started. I preached a short sermon on "How to be saved and how to know you're saved", and then I asked people who wanted to become Christians to stand up and come forward, emphasizing that only those who really meant business with God and were sincerely seeking Him should do so. I was staggered by the response – the entire congregation got out of their seats! Everyone was crying out for God – there was not one rebel or dissident voice. God had captured them all. Even the paralyzed man lying the aisle was trying to get up. The Lord was working in a mighty, miraculous way. In places like Malaysia and Zululand I had seen entire villages and towns come to meetings, but I had never before seen anything like this in Britain. When an entire congregation comes weeping to the altar, we can be sure that we are in the midst of a revival!

After all the people had been given a free Gospel or Bible to read and the Christian counsellors had got to work among them, I went down to minister to the paralyzed man. In his eyes you could see his pain and sadness, but you could also see hope. Hundreds of people were watching, wondering what God was going to do. The nurses stood aside, not knowing what to expect. I laid hands on the man, and I could feel the power of God flowing into his body. Everyone in the auditorium was with me, wanting that man to be healed; all doubts had flown, and the atmosphere was electric. Within seconds he was up on his feet! I tried to lend a hand, but he didn't need my help. The onlookers gasped with astonishment. The man was joyfully pushing his way through the crowd, making for the doors. "It's wonderful!" he was shouting amidst the loud applause. People who an hour ago had known nothing about Christ were now cheering and praising God. Although we were from such mixed backgrounds, we were all one in Christ. The man jumped and danced his way out of the building. That was the last I saw of him that afternoon. The nurses gathered up their bags and coats and rushed after him. He went home on the bus rather than in an ambulance car! Later two ambulance men came to collect him, but were astonished to find that he had already left the meeting unaided. One of them remarked, "This is a real church!" Today the man who was once paralyzed drives his car around Birmingham. He is a living miracle. Since that time the Aston Christian Centre has expanded by leaps and bounds, making a great impact upon central Birmingham.

Revival in the Highlands

Recently I was involved in a mission in Inverness, the gateway to the Scottish Highlands. Many Christians had warned me that the people of this region would not take kindly to anything untraditional. However, as always I preached the "old" Gospel – the true Gospel, which is as true today as it was when it was first preached. The meetings were held in the auditorium of the town's best hotel. The first meeting was very encouraging. The local folk who attended actually enjoyed it – in their previous experience services had always been things which had to be endured rather than enjoyed! I based my message on Ephesians 1:7, "in him we have redemption through his blood, the forgiveness of sins". Many people came forward to the front of the hall to kneel and ask forgiveness – some of them wept as they did so. I laid hands on the sick, and there was a rich manifestation of God's power – the Holy Spirit was with us!

A short, deep-voiced man named Tommy asked for prayer. He was a very familiar figure in the town and had been blind for six years. "If only I could see a little, it would be marvellous," he said. I immediately warmed to this man, who seemed so humble and appreciative. I prayed for him, and seconds later he saw a flash of light. His sight had been restored! Then he was no longer quiet and reserved but was praising God. Even the most tongue-tied get excited when God works in their lives! The people in the hall were impressed, and some of them even applauded. The next day Tommy walked down Inverness High Street, waving to people he knew and enjoying sights he had not seen for years – the sunshine, the trees, the beautiful river, the old churches, the majestic hills. His healing caused a sensation!

The next six meetings of the campaign were packed out, and hundreds came to the Lord. Revival had come to Inverness. Today there is a thriving church there which is winning many converts in the town and the surrounding villages and making a great mark on that part of the Highlands.

Revival in Penzance

I have seen revival come to the Scottish Highlands, and I have also seen it come to the other end of the nation – to Cornwall. A short while ago I led a crusade at Penzance. The church which had invited my colleagues and I to go there was tiny, but nevertheless the town was shaken by the campaign. The meetings were held in a redundant Methodist church. The place was two-thirds full on the first night. On subsequent nights we were packed out and people were queueing in the streets to get in. Great miracles of healing took place. A lady with a paralyzed spine was instantly healed. Lame people walked, deaf people regained their hearing and the blind were able to see. A BBC reporter came to one of the meetings. Afterwards he interviewed me. "We have seen incredible scenes here today, Reverend Banks," he said. "What is your explanation of all this? How is it that people are healed and the blind see?" I replied, "What is happening here is proof that Jesus Christ is alive and can do the same things He did in biblical times." The interview was broadcast three times in Cornwall and Devon.

The church became too small for the crowds, of whom 80% were not normally churchgoers. A large part of the population of Penzance was touched. As I walked the streets of the town during the day for a breath of fresh air, people greeted me on every side – they were folk who had been to the meetings. The whole area was alive with revival. Hundreds of people were saved and healed. The main Cornish newspaper carried an article about the revival on its front page. God's work continues in the county with great growth and success.

"The Healing Church" in Norwich

Mount Zion Church in Nelson Street, Norwich, is now probably the largest church in Norfolk. God has done many amazing miracles there in recent years, and it has become known as "the Healing Church". Hundreds have been converted at the yearly missions which I lead there. This church is witnessing a remarkable visitation of God. It has grown in numbers so rapidly that it has had to move into a huge new building.

Recently Anglia TV produced a late-night feature including interviews of people who had been healed at the church. One of them was Stan Skedge. He used to be crippled and lived in severe pain. No amount of medical help could do anything for him. His wife happened to see a newspaper advertisement about one of the campaigns at Mount Zion Church. She had heard that a lot of people had been healed there and believed that it could happen for her husband too. He was sceptical about what he called "faith healing" and was at first unwilling to go. But his wife and his sister were so persistent that eventually he gave in and agreed to go to one of the meetings. He sat passively through the service, unimpressed by what he saw and longing to go home again. But his wife and sister encouraged him to go forward for healing, so reluctantly he did. He was the last one in a long line of sick people, but eventually hands were laid on him and he was prayed for. He felt nothing at the time and went home just as he had come, in pain. But when he got home he found that for the first time in years he could get his socks off with ease. From that time his condition improved rapidly, and he is now healthy. Since then he has been baptized, and now he and his family are following the Lord faithfully.

Another person who was interviewed by Anglia TV was a lady named Maude who came to one of the meetings in a wheelchair. She found the service very long and tiring. Also, since she was virtually housebound she was not used to being among people, she so found the crowds, the singing and the clapping rather intimidating. She got so nervous that she asked her husband to take her home. But then a kindly steward talked with her and persuaded her to stay till the end of the service. She was then prayed for and was soon out of her wheelchair, overjoyed and dancing in the aisle! Her testimony has astounded her local area and has turned many to Christ. Hundreds of thousands saw her on TV and were amazed to find that God still works in supernatural power today. Now Maude walks unaided to the church services and never has to use her wheelchair. She spends her time helping the sick and aged.

Delivered from schizophrenia

Mrs Bibby had endured the terrible mental torture of schizophrenia for eighteen years. She had a constant headache and frequently heard voices. She had tried everything – spiritualism, alcohol, ouija. She had been under a psychiatrist and had spent long periods in hospital. But nothing ever did her the slightest good. She and her husband were so desperate that they were considering committing suicide. One day she was sitting watching her husband light the fire. He used newspaper to kindle it, and happened to drop a copy of the local paper on the carpet next to his wife. Something in it caught her eye. "I want to go there," she said. He didn't know what she was talking about, so she added, "Pick up that paper and read that advert to me." He did. It was about the healing crusade which was going to be held in Hulme. For some reason she had been drawn to the advert and knew with absolute certainty that she must go to one of the meetings.

But for about a week after that she was so ill that she couldn't leave the house, and in the end her husband, who was at his wit's end, told her that he couldn't cope any more. She must either go to the crusade or go back into hospital. She very nearly didn't make it – it took them all day to get her ready to go to the church. Once they got there she was so afraid that she twice tried to run out. But her husband supported her, and eventually she got into the line of people wanting healing. When she reached the front I read the details of her illness, which someone had written down for her on a card.

I said to her, "Jesus is going to heal you tonight. Do you believe that?"

"Yes," she replied.

You see, in spite of her awful illness, her fear and her confusion, Mrs Bibby had just a little bit of faith – enough faith to put her trust in Jesus. In effect she was saying, "Jesus, I don't know You, I've never really understood who You are before, but tonight I am willing to entrust myself to You." And God responded to her faith. When I laid my hands on her the headache lifted, the voices vanished and she received something she had never before known – perfect peace. Praise be to God! She was healed of schizophrenia that night, and it has never returned. Mrs Bibby's little bit of faith was the beginning of a whole new life of faith. She experienced the miraculous healing power of God, and now she's a changed woman. Today she and her husband enjoy the continuing exhilaration of living for Jesus.

In the present revival we are seeing many wonderful deliverances like this. People are being freed from demonic possession, despair, fear, anxiety and suicidal thoughts; they are being released from the power of Satan by the power of the Living God.

A writer is freed from agoraphobia

It is estimated that agoraphobia grips about half a million people in Britain to some degree. Over 100,000 of these people are acute cases: they cannot even go out their own front door. They live in dread and anxiety, unable to enjoy the sunshine, the countryside, going shopping, visiting friends or going on holiday. A certain highly successful lady writer suffered from this terrible condition. She was a famous name and her books sold all over the world, but she hadn't been out of her own house for twenty years. She was quite happy working at home, and she could even look out of the windows. But as soon as she tried to step outside a frantic, trembling spirit would overtake her.

A friend of hers went to one of the meetings which my colleagues and I were holding in a large football ground in South London. She had gone out of mere curiosity but had been touched by the stirring Holy Ghost atmosphere and had seen miracle after miracle. She managed to persuade her writer friend to agree to go to one of the meetings.

On the night the writer was dressed and ready to go when her friend called for her. The writer held on tightly to her friend as they went out the front door. Immediately she was terrified. She wept, digging her nails into her friend's arm. As they reached the garden gate she cried, "Take me back! Take me back!" To the waiting cabby's amazement her friend dragged her to the car, pushed her in and slammed the door shut. Then she got in herself and told him, "Drive fast! There'll be an extra five pounds for you if you get us to the football ground quickly!"

The cabby had never driven so fast in his life! All the way the writer was screaming and pleading with her friend, "Let's go home! Let's turn around!" Soon they were at the football ground, but she didn't want to get out of the car. She was in such a terrible state that her friend was beginning to regret taking her away from her home. "How is she going to be able to sit through the service in the stadium?" she thought. "I think I've made a big mistake bringing her here."

At that moment a burly steward arrived on the scene, wondering why the taxi's passengers had not got out. The writer's friend slowly wound down the window and in a whisper told the steward what the problem was. Quickly he went round to the other door, opened it, pulled the writer out and literally carried her through the gates of the stadium, while she cried frantically. Her friend hurriedly paid the cabby and then tried to catch up with the enthusiastic steward.

She found them both a few minutes later, and was amazed by what she saw. The writer was sitting in a seat near the front, and she looked calm and placid. As soon as she had passed through the gates God's Spirit had come upon her. She had been pacified by the holy, prayerful, peaceful, powerful atmosphere which pervaded the stadium. She sat through the service without a shudder or a worry, just as if she had never suffered from agoraphobia. She heard me preach and then came forward with hundreds of others to publicly receive Jesus as her Saviour. She talked with a Christian counsellor for a while and then went home without fear. She had actually enjoyed the evening at the football ground! She had been delivered from the bondage of agoraphobia. The next day she amazed her maid by getting on a bus and going shopping. She has been well ever since. She now goes on holiday, enjoys social functions, visits her friends and family and lives a normal life.

An atheist gets "a brand new spine"

Bill was a successful Lancashire businessman. He had come from a poor working-class background but, possessing confidence and ambition, he had worked hard and had done very well for himself. But then tragedy struck his life: he had an accident which left him with a cracked spine. It would not heal, and there was nothing the doctors could do for him except prescribe pain-killing tablets. Even with these he still suffered terrible pain. Then one day his niece, whom he had not seen for some time, called to see him. She had recently married, and he had heard that she had "gone religious". Bill was very fond of her, because she had such a sweet, sunny personality, but he couldn't understand why such a nice girl with such good looks would want to "go that way". Actually she had become a Christian and was telling everyone about Jesus. Some people thought she had "gone overboard with religion". Knowing how sick Bill was, she offered to take him to the healing crusade which was happening in a nearby church. Many people were getting healed at the meetings, she said. Bill reminded her that he was "not a scrap religious". He was an atheist and had hardly ever been inside a church in his life. He didn't understand "religion" and frankly had no interest in it at all. However, the thought that he might be able to get rid of his pain at the meeting and the fact that it was his favourite niece who was inviting him persuaded him to go.

The meeting was packed out, and the love, sincerity and genuineness of the Christians there moved him. He was soundly converted that night. After hands had been laid on him the pain in his spine vanished. He went home and took off his spinal jacket, and never wore it again. When his spine was X-rayed later it was found that it had healed completely. "You have a brand new spine," the amazed doctor told him. He sometimes brings his spinal jacket to church meetings as a trophy of God's healing power.

Born blind, but now able to see!

I was once preaching for a few nights in a northern town. The attendance at the meetings was a little disappointing. About thirty people were coming to Christ at each meeting and there were some definite healings, but the sort of breakthrough which I had seen elsewhere in the country was not in evidence. However, God did one truly amazing miracle there. One evening a blind elderly lady was led in to the meeting by some friends. They told me that she had been born completely blind. She had been very keen to come to the meeting and believed that God would touch her eyes and enable her to see. This was quite a challenge to me. This lady had not lost her sight – she had been born blind!

A little nervous, I went over to her to pray for her.

She was a sweet, humble person, and her face looked so hopeful. I prayed a long, hard prayer for her. Finally I finished and took my hands off her. "I can see strips of light up there!" she exclaimed in great excitement, pointing behind me. I thought she was just seeing it in her mind. "Up there, up there!" she cried. I turned around and noticed that the light from a streetlamp was shining through some long, narrow windows high up in the wall behind me. She really could see! I prayed for her again and again, expecting her to receive perfect vision there and then, but her sight did not improve any more that night. As she was driven home she saw moving lights – these were the streetlamps.

Before long the lady gained full vision. Her story was so amazing that she was interviewed on TV. As she walked in her garden, admiring the spring flowers, she told the interviewer that God had healed her after a lifetime of blindness. She said it was a great miracle of Jesus. Hundreds of thousands of people heard her wonderful testimony.

The "miracle woman"

A young man named Raymond House, who lived in Mansfield in Nottinghamshire, was walking home one evening. His eyes were so filled with tears that he could hardly see where he was going. He was soon going to lose the light of his life, his beloved Mum. She was dying of cancer of the liver. She lay on her bed at home, almost as thin as a skeleton, with at most only a few weeks to live. As Raymond came to the corner shop near his home some bright colour in its window caught his eye. Above the tomatoes, lettuces, cucumbers, apples and oranges was an attractive poster. The words on it hit him like a bolt of lightning: "Miracle Healing Crusade to Mansfield". He could not believe his eyes – surely this was a dream. He read on – the meetings were being held in a large church on the edge of town. This was the very last night of the crusade. He ran home as fast as his legs would carry him. He told his Dad, who listened with rapt attention.

"Well, it can't do any harm trying it, son," he mused. "It seems a coincidence – almost fate. Here we are, desperate, nowhere to turn to, then this turns up!" Making up his mind, he said, "We'll go. It will be a job getting your mother in the car, but we'll manage. We'll take plenty of blankets and keep her warm. Go back to the shop and write the details down – we don't want to end up at the wrong church."

The House family arrived at the service late. They had lost their way in the dark, and then they hadn't been able to find a parking space, since all the streets near the church had been chock-a-block with cars belonging to people who had come to the meeting. Some stewards helped Mr House to get his wife into the church. At the end of the service my colleagues and I prayed for her. She was instantly saved and her pain vanished. She still felt weak, but with some help she managed to walk out of the church. On the next Sunday she and her husband came to church to give thanks to God. Today she is completely well and there is no trace of cancer in her liver. In fact it has completely regenerated – she has a new liver! The local hospital call her "the miracle woman".

CHAPTER 6

Trophies of Grace

As cold waters to a thirsty soul, so is [God's] good news.

(King Solomon)

In the move of God which has been happening over the past two or three years many "trophies of grace" (to use an old evangelical word) have been raised up. These are outstanding conversions from totally secular backgrounds. People who were at rock bottom – seduced by Satan and destroyed by the world, the flesh and the devil – have become radiant believers and overcomers. Their faith is not a seven-day wonder; rather, their lives have been transformed by God. They are now growing in faith, worshipping God and committed to the local body of Christ. Not all of them have been brought to Christ through a revival crusade or mission. Some of them have found Jesus as the Holy Spirit has struck them down in their homes or on the streets. Some have been saved through a revived Christian loved one or through the ministry of one of the local fellowships which have come alive in recent days. Below are the stories of just a few of the very many trophies of grace which we have seen in the present revival.

He found peace in Christ

This is the testimony of Eric Eddles from Portsmouth:

"I followed the Guru Marasha Yoga, whom the Beatles sought help from years ago. I was deeply into it. I was mesmerized by this man and his "peace" philosophy. I had a deep need of peace, but no-one – not the Guru or medical psychologists or anyone else – could help me to find it. I had also suffered constant headaches for three years – a splitting pain, day and night. I could not live in happiness with my family. I didn't know what to do with myself, because I was suffering so much in mind and body. I decided to kill myself, my wife and our two sons. I had planned it all out and was on my way to carry out this foul deed. Then I saw a poster advertising a "Divine Healing Crusade"; then I saw another and another. I was handed a leaflet about it, and my wife had one through the letter-box. Portsmouth was plastered with the news that someone called Melvin Banks was coming to the Central Hall. I was attracted by the colourful literature and the stories of miracles. I had thought that no-one – not even the Church – believed in that sort of thing any more, but here was someone claiming that miracles still happened today.

"I decided to go to the meeting instead of killing my family – I thought it might just work for me. My wife Olive came with me on my motorbike. We arrived late at the crowded auditorium. The noise was unbearable – all that clapping and loud singing! After an hour it became too much for me and I decided to leave. I thought they were all mad! Then a steward stopped me and suggested that I stay just a little longer. He told me that Melvin Banks would soon speak and would then pray for the sick. Reluctantly I agreed to stay.

"When the people started to queue up for the 'laying on of hands', I thought it was all a con trick. Blind people said they could see, people who were supposed to have been crippled walked without crutches, deaf people threw their hearing aids away. 'They must all be paid by him to do it,' I thought.

"Then Melvin Banks laid his hands on me and prayed for me, and I fell over. I had never experienced anything like it! It was like a bolt of power out of the blue. I was free from pain and demonic disturbances. I began to cry to Jesus. I felt new as I repented. I did not know what it meant, but I knew I had to say sorry to God. I was broken . . .

"God's light flooded me, Scriptures were read to me, and I went home a brand new man. I was free from the occult, from hatred, hurt and emptiness. I was filled with joy and purpose. Everlasting life had begun. I did not understand all the doctrine until later, as I did not know the Bible. But I have come to love it. I now follow Christ and witness for Him in the dockyards where I work. I also hold prayer meetings for my workmates in the lunch-breaks. My wife and family now follow the Lord as well. We will never be the same again."

Freed from drug addiction

Life was meaningless for Steve Roberts, a young engineer living in Gosport in Hampshire. "At my first job I saw men who had spent forty-five years in engineering, only to be rewarded for their labours by a short retirement and early death," he writes. Faced with this hard reality, he adopted the philosophy of putting the least into life and getting the most out of it, looking for kicks in as many ways as possible. He played drums in a rock band, bought a motorbike, grew long hair, drank heavily and took drugs. "I progressed from cannabis to speed and LSD in my search for pleasure and wisdom," he says, "but something deep within me knew that drugs weren't right. But what alternative was there?"

One day Steve met an ex-drug addict who told him how Jesus had freed him from drugs and given him meaning in life. "He talked about Jesus as if He was an old friend whom he knew and loved," recalls Steve. However, he lost contact with this Christian and got deeper and deeper into the drugs subculture. "Lawlessness was what our life was all about, and we used to look upon the Hell's Angels with a sort of awe."

Years passed, and Steve withdrew from biking so as to spend more time on his music. Then an invitation to attend a church meeting brought back memories of the Christian who had spoken to him about Jesus years before. Steve took the plunge and agreed to go. He found that the church meeting was full of people who talked about Jesus the same way as the ex-addict had. Steve didn't feel at ease that night. "I left knowing that I had to make my choice – between heaven and hell, Jesus and drugs." Thankfully he chose Jesus. "When I gave my life to Jesus I didn't feel the 'high' I used to get from drugs, but I knew I was truly free. The happiness I have now does not change with circumstances, because it is a deep, eternal happiness. I no longer fear death or the pain of living a pointless existence in the world." Steve, aged twenty-seven, is now happily married to Jean, and together they belong to a Christian fellowship.

The journey of a lifetime for a Hell's Angel

"I was a man of violence. I drank a lot, I rode my motorbike wildly and I was the sort of person you just wouldn't want to know. I was initiated into a breakaway group of the Hell's Angels called the Kick-Start Angels. I was nicknamed 'the Duke'. In bloody fights and mad bike and car chases I came within inches of death many times. I knocked people unconscious and sometimes almost killed them. My whole life was a mess and was getting worse and worse. I drank so much that I began to get shakes and tremours – the early stages of alcoholism. Some of my mates burned a family Bible which I had found. For some reason this apalled me, and from that time I knew that there was something wrong with my life.

"Some friends and I set out on a trip across Europe on our bikes, looking for kicks. In Rome one of my friends, a former Roman Catholic, wanted to go and see the Sistine Chapel. I wasn't interested in God, but I went with him because I thought the architecture and art would be worth seeing. Inside the church, as I stood looking at a huge fifty-foot-high crucifix, I had a kind of vision. I felt I had in my hand the hammer which had driven the nails into Jesus' feet and hands. I told myself I was having these thoughts because I was a carpenter by trade. But then I felt I was looking not at a statue but at the real Jesus. He loved me so much – how could I do this to Him? He had never meant anything to me before, but now I broke down and wept with sorrow and shame. I did not know how to pray, but I knew there and then that Jesus was 100% God. I went out of the Sistine Chapel a changed man – changed not by mere statues and paintings but by an encounter with the Living Christ. I didn't understand much about all this at the time – I knew no doctrine or theology, *but I knew Christ.*

"My friends were very surprised by the change in me, but they were not antagonistic. From that time on I found that God was real to me, that He was changing me from a man of anger, hatred and bitterness into a man of love, joy, peace and concern for others. I truly repented of my sins and surrendered and dedicated my life to Jesus Christ. All the drinking, gang warfare and wild living vanished.

"I have made the journey of a lifetime, out of the Hell's Angels and into Christ's Bride. I'm going all the way with our Lord to heaven. God is pouring out revival increasingly on His people – I'm going to be part of it, I'm going to be part of the army that is going to take the whole country for King Jesus!"

A pop musician has a new song in his heart

From the age of fifteen Danny Owen's ambition was to become a pop superstar. But he never made it. He recorded several albums and singles, but they weren't hugely successful. He appeared on TV several times in programmes like *Sumertime Special*, *Search for a Star*, *Dr Who* and *Eastenders*, but he only ever had small parts. He became very bitter and depressed because he had not become a superstar. He started drinking a lot and his doctor prescribed valium and librium for him. He also started being unfaithful to his wife. "I was just an empty person waiting to be filled by something," he says. Visits to clairvoyants and mediums failed to provide him with any answers. Then he saw an advert in a national newspaper for a book, entitled *Power for Living*. He sent off for it. "It basically said that there were only two paths in life – God's path and the world's. It also mentioned Jesus, who I didn't know a lot about. It explained who He was, what He came to do and what He could do for me."

Soon after receiving the book, Danny had to go to Sweden on business. When he was in Stockholm he decided to go to a church. "When I walked into the church I found it was full of love, joy, happiness and peace. It was then that I asked the Lord to come into my life." In order to do that, Danny had to admit that he had been going his own way and shutting God out of his life. "I told the Lord I wanted to turn away from my rotten past and my rotten future." The next day Danny felt like a different person. "It was one of those overnight jobs with me. I said, 'Come on in,' and He did, and He changed me." Danny discovered that his depression had lifted and that he no longer needed to drink. "When I got back home my wife threw me out – she thought I had gone crazy! It's a long story, but in the end the Lord put us back together again." Danny's wife and three children have now all become Christians. So too have his parents and parents-in-law. "To me, that's a miracle," says Danny. He is still amazed by what God has done for him. He says knowing that you belong to the Living God is "the greatest thing in the world".

A new beginning for a suicidal man

"When I was a lad my family attended the local Baptist church in Kings Sutton, a village near Banbury. I was sent to Sunday school and when I was seventeen I made a half-hearted Christian commitment and was baptized. For a few years after that I taught in the Sunday school. Then I started going out with a girl and so began to go to church less. When I was twenty-one I got married, and my wife and I had three lovely daughters. But our marriage ended twelve years later when my wife went off with my best friend. A year later I remarried, but this marriage also ended in divorce four years later. I then went to live with my mother again, but I didn't bother to go to church, even though my mother's house was just opposite the Baptist church I had attended as a child. Two years later I married for the third time and moved to Leamington Spa. I thought that this time I was happily married and that everything was going to be all right. But five years later things started to go wrong and my wife wanted a divorce.

"I became very depressed and went to talk to some friends, but they didn't really want to know about my troubles. A few weeks later, on the Monday before Easter, I tried again to talk to someone, but they too weren't really interested. I was at my very lowest. When I got home I said to myself, "I've had enough." I got a glass of water, went upstairs to the bedroom, closed the door and put the wardrobe, dressing table and bed against it. I was taking tablets for my depression and I swallowed a whole bottle of them. After a few minutes the room started to go round – I don't remember much after that. My wife came looking for me but found that she could not get into the bedroom. With some help from our neighbours she managed to get in. I was rushed to Warwick Hospital, where I was pumped out. I was then transferred to Leamington Hospital. I don't remember much of Tuesday. When my wife came to see me on Wednesday I asked her if we could start again. She said "No." I went to the toilet and just cried and cried until the nurses came and calmed me down. On Thursday night I couldn't sleep. I looked around for something to read. There were no magazines or papers; all I had to read was a Gideon Bible. I picked it up and it fell open at John 3:16. I know now that this was the hand of the Lord at work. I read the verse and it really hit me between the eyes. That God could send His Son to save a sinner like me – someone who had tried to take his own life! I read some other passages and then I closed the Bible. As I did so the light around my bed got brighter and brighter. I could feel the presence of God with me. I just fell to my knees and asked Jesus to come into my life and to forgive all my sins – especially my attempted suicide.

Since then things have not always been easy, but with the Lord in my life I have always got through. I have joined a thriving local church, where I teach in the Sunday school and help run the football team. I must say I am very glad that on that Thursday night in the hospital there was a Bible next to my bed!

A Great Train Robber's tracks lead to miracles. After preaching in a western town, as I was in the carpark ready to leave, an excited steward told how one of the converts was a former Great Train Robber. Fourteen years in prison had induced asthma, but news of miracles had drawn the man to his first ever Gospel meeting. From that day on the dynamics of the Almighty transformed him. He found fellowship and pardon and lost the asthma. Nothing is too hard for the Lord!

CHAPTER 7

The Revival is a "Re-Bible"

If we live the way the Bible teaches, we shall be ignited.

(George Verwer)

A Christian from South India, where there had been great revival and growth in the Church, was once visiting North India, where the Church was less flourishing. He was trying to explain to a local believer there about the wonderful revival in the South. The northerner could not understand the meaning of the word "revival", so the southerner told him, "We are having a great re-Bible in the South!" Really he was quite right to say this, for a Christian revival is always a return to the Book of Books – the Holy Bible. There is no revival without strong biblical proclamation, without ardent love for God's Holy Word. In the present revival in the UK the Church is rediscovering the Word of God.

The Book of Books

God's Word is the only thing that can answer the cry from man's heart. The human condition – man's despair, crisis, emptiness, sadness, loneliness, lostness, thirst and hunger of heart – can only be solved by the Living Word.

God's Word is for today; He has not changed His rulings. Just as the Word of the Lord came to the Old Testament prophets, so it comes to us today as the hope of mankind. As Dr J. Wesley White put it, "The world hopes for the best; the Christian has the best hope." The Bible gives us that hope!

If you want to know what God thinks, read the Bible. If you want to know what God does with men and women when they die, read the Bible. If you want to know how to get a revival, read the Bible. If you want to know what God's plans for you are, what God says today, what God is going to do with the world in the future, you must read the Bible.

Hold up your Bible in your hand – there you have the thoughts of God. If you live in the Word, you can walk daily with Abraham, Isaac, Jacob, Elijah, Isaiah, Peter, Paul and the other prophets. Through this book you can take the hand of Jesus and walk with Him through His earthly ministry as recorded in the Gospels of Matthew, Mark, Luke and John. You can think God's thoughts – you can think as He does about salvation, healing, forgiveness, mercy, deliverance, love, goodness, morality, eternal life, things to come, and many other wonderful things. "Blessed is the man who does not walk in the counsel of the wicked or stand in the way of sinners or sit in the seat of mockers. But his delight is in the law [or Word] of the Lord, and on his law he meditates day and night" (Psalm 1:1-2).

Jesus Himself laid great emphasis on God's Word (which was just the Old Testament in His time). In the Gospel of Matthew He says five times, "Have you not read . . .?" – meaning the Scriptures. He dealt with such matters as marriage, justice, religion and life after death by quoting from them.

The blueprint for our lives

We are directed by the Holy Scriptures; God guides us by His Word. As Paul says, it is written for "teaching, rebuking, correcting and training in righteousness, so that the man of God may be thoroughly equipped for every good work" (2 Timothy 3:16-17).

Let the Word of God be the blueprint for your life. George Muller said, "The vigour of our spiritual life will be in exact proportion to the place held by the Bible in our life and thoughts." Our spirituality can be judged by our attitude to the Scriptures. It may be said that God's attitude to us is determined by our attitude to His Word. He has said, "This is the one I esteem: he who is humble and contrite in spirit, and trembles at my word" (Isaiah 66:2).

Paul says, "from the very beginning God decided that [we] should become like his Son" (Romans 8:29, LB). God uses a variety of means to achieve this goal in our lives, and one of the most important of those means is His Word. When we read and meditate upon the Bible a spiritual force and power which has been breathed into it by God flows into our spirits and makes us the kind of people He wants us to be. An old saying goes, "All other books were written for our information, but the Bible was written for our transformation."

Augustine was brought up by a godly Christian mother, but he ran away from home and went to live in sin in the city of Milan. One day, as he was walking down the street, he heard some children singing a popular song of the day: "Take up and read, take up and read . . ." Although the song was about something else altogether, it triggered his memories of the teaching from the

Scriptures which he had received from his mother. Returning to his lodgings, he happened to discover that his mother had hidden a scroll in his belongings before he had left home. It was a portion of the Scriptures. He read it and was born again. It changed him; he became a new person in Christ through the mighty Word.

We are always learning things from the Bible. I read new thoughts in it or am inspired in a new way by it almost daily, even though I may have read the same verses dozens or even hundreds of times before. They light up with a fresh revelation, a living, inspiring anointing.

The Word of God was not written just for the people who first read it, but for all people in all times. The Word is of eternal meaning and significance. Jesus said, "Heaven and earth will pass away, but my words will never pass away" (Matthew 24:35). That verse is gold-dust! Do you realize that the words of Jesus are more reliable and dependable than the ground you walk on? You don't expect that to give way beneath your feet at any moment; the words of Jesus are even more rock solid! If we base our lives on them, we will be living on the firm rock of which He spoke: "everyone who hears these words of mine and puts them into practice is like a wise man who built his house on a rock. The rain came down, the streams rose, and the winds blew and beat against that house; yet it did not fall, because it had its foundation on the rock" (Matthew 7:24-25).

Every time you read the Word it enters into you, and there it begins to create faith. Through the reading of the Word our faith gets big. It is the DIY book that gives you faith.

When you believe the Word of God, that Word can then be translated into action – God's action in your life and in the world around you. The Bible stresses the importance of hearing the words of God and then believeing them: "Lay hold of my words with all your heart; keep my commands and you will live . . . Listen, my son, accept what I say . . . pay attention to what I say; listen closely to my words. Do not let them out of your sight, keep them within your heart; for they are life to those who find them and health to a man's whole body" (Proverbs 4:4, 10, 20-22).

Read the Bible every day. I try to read eight chapters a day, although I don't always keep to that rule – sometimes I read more than eight chapters!

The Word of God and revival

The Anglican theologian John Stott has said recently, "Nothing is more important for the health of the Church than the recovery of biblical preaching." It is certainly true that a crucial element in the present revival is an emphasis on the Word. We are teaching our young (and older) preachers, workers and helpers that Christian superficiality is not good enough. Instead we must be people of the Word! There has been some exciting church growth in the last ten years or so, but there has also been a dreadful fall-out rate. This has been caused by the carnal living of Christians, and this in turn has been caused by a lack of sound, authoritative, biblical preaching. Churches will only grow, flourish, overcome and live long if they are living on the Word of God. And the revival will only have a community-wide and nation-wide impact when *the Holy Spirit carries the Word of God home with power to the people's hearts.* This is what we are telling our leaders and people, and the message is beginning to bite. We tell them to *have confidence in the powerful Word of God*. Do not change the message, but become a better communicator of it. The biblical message is dynamic and life-changing. Make an uncompromizing commitment to all the truths of God in the Bible – the saving blood of Christ, true repentance, the imputed righteousness of Christ, faith, divine healing through the atonement, holiness of life, and the Second Coming of Christ.

It is said of the great preacher George Whitefield that he preached the Word of God in such sincerity and power that people actually fell down in a heap as he proclaimed it. As he drew vivid pictures and graphic descriptions from it the multitudes who heard him were held in breathless silence, except for the weeping and moaning of those under conviction. Lord Chesterfield said he "preached like a lion" and made the Bible so gripping that "you had to listen whether you wanted to or not. Its energy and power carried many off their legs; hearers were stripped of their apathy." That is the sort of preaching we need today!

It has been my experience, and the experience of the other preachers who are involved in the revival, that the more we preach the Word and make much of it, the more incredible, stunning, life-changing miracles we see. Where the Word is played down or lost in a welter of singing and dancing, where the Word is given only a passing reference and is forgotten because there is excessive emphasis on supernatural novelties and outward manifestations, there the impetus of the revival is lost. If we stop emphasizing the Word of God, the revival will wane, but if we keep on preaching the Word, I believe the whole of Britain can be saved.

As we go from town to town in the revival, proclaiming the glad tidings, shouting the good news, crying God's message, we see drunkards made sober, adulterers made pure, broken families reconciled, the bigoted and religious made humble, the respectable made better than they have ever been before – we see all this happening by the magnificent Word of God. We are plundering the devil's kingdom, releasing captives, opening blind eyes, driving out demons as old-fashioned, life-changing, Christlike faith is revived in our midst.

There is no land which is too hard for the Holy Spirit to work in, there is no country that is so closed to the Gospel that it cannot be opened, there is no church which is too dead to be revived. *The answer is the Word of God.* He has said, "Is not my word like fire . . . and like a hammer that breaks a rock in pieces?" (Jeremiah 23:29).

The Word of God is a powerful weapon. When we use it we can defeat the enemy. He is disarmed and overpowered when we declare, "It is written . . ." He is a weakling and a fake and is flattened by the Word. John wrote, "you are strong, and the word of God lives in you, and you have overcome the evil one" (1 John 2:14).

You must accept the absolute rule of this Book over your life. This is the attitude which is changing people in this current revival. We must do as Paul and his partners did: "We demolish arguments and every pretension that sets itself up against the knowledge of God, and we take captive every thought to make it obedient to Christ" (2 Corinthians 10:5). Don't bring your mind to the Word, but bring the Word to your mind. Put your thoughts under the authority of the Word of God.

The Word brings the power and the Kingdom of God

to us now, today. Jesus said, "The kingdom of God is near" (Mark 1:15). It is here on earth, it is amongst us, it is here already. Paul wrote, "For he has rescued us from the dominion of darkness and brought us into the kingdom of the Son he loves" (Colossians 1:13). If you have been saved, you have been freed from the enemy's kingdom and brought into Christ's Kingdom. You can have and enjoy the blessings of that Kingdon now, for the King of glory has brought it down to us. That Kingdom can be yours by the power of the Word of God. When Jesus came to Lazarus' tomb and said, "Lazarus, come out!" Martha and Mary were seeing the Word of God in action. That Word brought the dead back to life, it brought the Kingdom down to earth. The Word of God can do the same for us today.

It is not enough to have the mere printed words of the Bible. Samuel Coleridge said, "The Bible without the Spirit is like a sundial by moonlight." George Fox said to Oliver Cromwell, "What does it matter that we have the Scriptures if we have lost the Spirit who wrote them?" Revival comes about through a return of the Holy Spirit on His proclaimed Word. This living Word has the power to ignite society. The Holy Spirit working within you brings the written Word alive. It seems that it is addressed personally to you – it has relevance in your life.

I like the story of the highly effective Black preacher who was once asked what the secret of his revival preaching was. He replied, "I read myself full, I think myself clear, I pray myself hot, then I let myself go!" Note that he started with the Word. *Read yourself full, soak yourself in the Book of Books.* Store up the Word of God in your mind. Become marked by a faith that believes God's promises, a humility that is not feigned but real, a fear of God which touches all your plans and actions; be fuelled by the divine commandments.

In the present revival God is using ordinary folk – bricklayers, insurance salesmen, secretaries, housewives, farmers, nurses, gas meter readers – to stir the society in which we live with the Word; He is using them to win souls and to break down the power of the enemy. God speaks through us, using our humble lips to proclaim His lovely truths. *The world is waiting to hear the glad sound of His words!*

Now thousands are looking beyond the drudgery, complacency, affluence, misery and boredom which have dominated their rat-race lives for years and are instead seeking God, living for His Word. That Word is a feast full of wonders, joy, glory, health, recovery, zest and life – all through our loving, living Lord Jesus Christ.

CHAPTER 8

A Revival of Gospel Preaching

The Gospel is nothing but a frozen asset, unless it is communicated.

(J. B. Phillips)

During the Restoration era, when evangelical and Puritan Christians were being persecuted, a law was passed in our land which made it illegal for anyone to preach the Gospel outside the confines of Anglican churches, and even there it could be preached only twice a week. One clergyman who was full of the Spirit of God went everywhere declaring Christ and winning souls. He was betrayed and was brought before his bishop. The bishop asked him if it were true that he was preaching the Gospel more than twice a week. The clergyman replied that the charge was untrue. The bishop remonstrated with him and asked him again. But the clergyman replied again, "No, bishop, I preach the Gospel only twice a week." The bishop asked him when he preached. With a twinkle in his eye the man of God said, "I preach only twice, sir – in season and out of season!"

At the present time we are witnessing a revival of that sort of preaching – preaching which is bold, biblical, apostolic and Christ-centred. Believers are going out into the world with the original Gospel message, not with a human message or mystical traditions. They are telling the Good News to whole villags, towns and cities – they are telling people about Christ's substitutionary death and cleansing blood.

Our preaching needs to be life-changing. A sermon should feed the souls of its hearers; it should stimulate their minds, make their hearts sing, renew their spirits and radically correct their lives. A sermon should give them the power to get through the next week.

During the funeral of King George V in 1937 a rather strange thing happened. The sceptre, crown and cross – the emblems of kingship – fell off the top of the coffin. The cross rolled into the gutter at the feet of a young sailor who was one of the guards accompanying the coffin on its route. The whole procession came to a halt. The crown and the sceptre were replaced, and the sailor picked up the cross. An Army colonel quickly ran up to him and told him, "Don't worry about putting the cross back on the coffin – we've got to get the procession moving again!" The young fellow replied, "But we can't have a crown without a cross, sir!" So the cross was duly replaced in its rightful position, above the crown and the sceptre. Similarly, it is true today that we cannot have a revival without the Cross – and it must be supreme, above everything else.

The traditionalists in the Church have *ritualized* the Cross. The evangelicals have *marginalized* it. The liberals have *rationalized* it. Most charismatics have *by-passed* it. But this present revival is a *return* to the Cross of our Lord Jesus Christ! The bleeding, suffering Lamb slain from the foundation of the world is pre-eminent! The heart of this revival is the finished work of Calvary. Jesus said, "I, when I am lifted up from the earth, will draw all men to myself"

(John 12:32). This is the secret of the revival: the Cross is the attraction.

One thing which the revival is clearly demonstrating is that what you preach Jesus to be, He will be! If you preach a limited Jesus, then He cannot be Himself. He doesn't save unless you preach that He is the Saviour. He doesn't heal unless you preach that He is the Healer. In the past many preachers have been guilty of stripping our precious Lord. Men once stripped Him before He was crucified; today unbelief strips Him of His power. In many a church He is no longer mighty to save and to heal.

In the revival we are returning to the Full Gospel. In this century there has been too much compromize in the Church. You can see it in every denomination. Ministers have cut corners, they have been afraid to speak out, they have forgotten the anointing of God, they have misused or neglected signs and wonders, they have denied that Jesus is the only way to the Father. We must preach the Full Gospel, and that Gospel says that only in Jesus is there salvation. Peter said, "Salvation is found in no-one else, for there is no other name under heaven given to men by which we must be saved" (Acts 4:12). Confucius said, "I know the way"; Hari Krishna said, "I see the way"; the Buddha said, "I am seeking the way"; the New Age Movement says, "Let's all travel together along the way". But Jesus said, "I am the way." He is exclusive.

If the Gospel is preached just as an idea, it makes no impact. But when it is preached under the power of the Holy Spirit a process then begins and something takes place. This is God's formula, and it produces results. When the Holy Spirit and Gospel preaching come together, there is an explosion of power. Divine energy is released. Paul called it *energemata* or "out-working energy". When such an explosion occurs the Gospel becomes news. When this heavenly force breaks upon us, there are extraordinary and highly interesting effects. There is revival – the graveyard atmosphere is gone! Meetings cease to be mere ritual. But this power is not a blind force – it is Jesus at work again!

The sign of a genuine revival is that hundreds and thousands of people recognize and acknowledge their sins, repent and in faith accept Jesus Christ as their Saviour and Lord. A person's salvation takes priority over his healing. We dare not reverse the biblical order.

The present revival is more than glorious supernatural experiences, imortant though those are. Such manifestations are vital, but there is something even more important – and that is repentance. What a difference it makes! The most important part of the revival is the lasting effect which the message of the Cross and the Resurrection has in the hearts and minds of believers and unbelievers alike. This repentance brings glory to our precious Lord Jesus Christ.

We in this country have a disaster of staggering proportions on our hands: *one million people go to hell every year*. Yet the great majority of church members, and even most evangelicals, show very little concern about rescuing these people. Thank God that in this revival there is a new passion among Christians for taking the message to the lost!

And what is that message – the message which is saving so many souls and changing countless lives in Britain today? Simply *Jesus* – we glorify Jesus, we preach His death and resurrection, we magnify His spotless and holy Name. This revival gets results not by using gimmicks or entertainment or pop music or showbiz or mass organization, but through the simple, powerful preaching of the Gospel. We have no new "in thing", no special new doctrine or idea. Many accuse us of preaching an old message, but we are proud of doing so. And this is the message: *Jesus died on the Cross so that we might not die. Those who believe in Him have passed from death to life.* One preacher asked me, "What is the theme of this new awakening?" I told him that it is the same as the theme of the revivals in which Paul preached: "nothing . . . except Jesus Christ and him crucified" (1 Corinthians 2:2).

While I was leading a crusade in a university city I received an invitation from the medical students at the University to come and prove that divine healing works today. Really it was more of a challenge than an invitation, since the students were very sceptical. The local TV people got to hear about it, and before the meeting they were outside the hall where it was to take place, interviewing the students as they went in. Most of their comments were negative. As I arrived at the packed hall I could feel that the atmosphere was very tense, and likely to turn rowdy. The attitude of the students was one of unbelief bordering on antagonism. As I appeared on the stage there was some derisive hooting, whistling and shouting. The two local pastors who were with me were clearly nervous. The TV cameras were now inside, filming the proceedings.

A student leader stood up and said a few introductory words about me and the purpose of this meeting. While he was speaking I was praying and thinking about what I should say to these young people. I had brought with me a lot of newspaper cuttings about the miracles which had happened in my crusades and some medical evidence concerning the healing of certain individuals. I was hoping to convince the students intellectually! But then I heard a voice in my heart saying, "Preach the Cross!" I didn't really want to do that – I had other plans. But then I heard the voice again: "Uplift the Cross!" I was still struggling within when the student leader came to the end of his introductions. "He is a daring preacher to accept our challenge; he need not have come," he said in conclusion.

As I stood up to speak the TV people pointed their cameras at me, doubtless expecting to be able to film some riotous scenes. There were some mocking cheers from the back, and then silence fell. I hardly knew how to start – that word from God had disorientated me. I could not get going for a moment, and I heard an anxious sigh coming from one of the pastors. He probably thought this little English preacher was going to make a fool of himself! My voice must have been very quiet as I started, for someone shouted "Speak up!" I lifted my head and grew more confident. Soon God was flashing thoughts and scriptures into my mind, one after another. I gave them some medical evidence and some testimonies, but my talk was dominated by that old message, that mighty 2,000-year-old fact of facts – the fact that Jesus bled and died for us. I told them that He suffered agony on the Cross so that we might be saved from our sins and healed from our sicknesses. For "He took up our infirmities and carried our diseases" (Matthew 8:17), and "by his wounds we are healed" (Isaiah 53:5). I told them that no tranquillizer or any other sort of pill could heal the soul, that no medical prescription could cure the heart's desperate spiritual illness. I told them that even when medical science could not cure someone, God could cure them through the power of the Cross and the blood of His Son.

I finished, and utter silence fell on the students. The TV crew looked around in dismay – there was no shouting or rioting for them to film. The lion had become a lamb. The wild spirits of the students had been tamed by the power which had been released at Golgotha. What a victory! The TV people interviewed some of the students after the meeting, and the mocking scepticism was now gone. God had touched them that night; He had quieted and convicted them, and doutless converted some of them.

In Withywood, Bristol, a huge, sprawling estate with little interest in spiritual things but with immense social problems, God broke through. Hundreds flocked to revival meetings. There is a great new light in the city.

There is the miracle of Pauline, freed from MS, and through that the conversion of her husband, which led to a lovely growing family church in Clevedon. Her story was carried to thousands of readers by a whole page in many West of England papers.

On South Humberside, beginning with only six folk, and virtually no interest in the local churches, hundreds crammed Gospel meetings. Six hundred and fifty people registered public commitment. We even had to call on the police to control the traffic. One officer spoke of "the joy of people leaving the services, and the sight of cured people going home well was so impressive."

In Portrush, Northern Ireland, people slept in their cars all day in order to get a seat in the hall. In Hittisleigh, Devon, a very small village, a prophecy eight years ago had told the dying church to move a side wall to be ready for extension, and to build a ramp outside for wheelchairs. Then in 1990, I preached in Hittisleigh for three nights. The BBC carried news of the revival and people flocked there. A hundred were converted, the blind saw, wheelchairs were left empty. It was the greatest revival since the chapel opened in 1903.

CHAPTER 9

A Heaven-Bombarding Revival

> Neither will I hide my face from you any more, for I have poured out my Spirit, God said.
>
> *(Ezekiel 39:29)*

Fervent prayer is one of the hallmarks of this present revival. Christians are bombarding heaven and seeing wonderful results. I am convinced that the revival we are seeing in isolated pockets in this country would be possible everywhere if people would dedicate themselves to believing prayer.

Those caught up in the revival are finding that prayer is giving them victory and protection from the enemy's attacks. It is bringing them great joy and peace amidst pressures, obstacles, misunderstanding and opposition. They are finding that they are growing through prayer and meditation.

The present revival is happening because groups of godly men and women have been weeping in repentance before the Lord and have been earnestly praying that He will visit this land again, that our generation will see signs and wonders. They have taken to heart the promise which God made long ago: "if my people, who are called by my name, will humble themselves and pray and seek my face and turn from their wicked ways, then I will hear from heaven and will forgive their sin and will heal their land" (2 Chronicles 7:14). So now prayer is beginning to lift us up towards the mountain-top of victory. The firstfruits of revival are evident in many different places. The only force which can combat the rising tide of evil in our land is the Holy Spirit of the Almighty God, and we are now seeing His Spirit at work in response to prayer.

I am finding that through a few lives placed utterly at His disposal God can move mountains. When God's people seek His face and pray the Lord gets His big bulldozers out and the mountains really start to collapse!

Matthew Henry said, "When God intends great mercy for his people, the first thing he does is to set them a-praying." No prayer – no power, no progress.

God longs to give us revival, if we first repent and pray. Arthur Wallis wrote, "The longing for revival has its source in the heart of God. So when we pray for it we don't have to conquer God's reluctance but simply grasp his willingness." We have been doing just that!

A few years ago I had a very memorable discussion with Eric Hutchings, one of the outstanding British evangelists of this century. "Melvin," he said, "two or three years ago I would never have made such a confession to anyone, but I have not been the man of prayer I ought to have been. Something has happened to me. I've just returned from Korea. Do you know that they hold prayer meetings between 4.30 and 5.30 every morning? I went to some of those meetings – I heard people in their thousands *praying before going to work*, and to a hard day's work as well. I told someone about this yesterday, and do you know what they said? They said it was all trivial, wishy-washy and skin deep! I told them that if it's trivial, wishy-washy Christianity to get out of bed at 4.00 every morning in sub-zero temperatures to pray, then we want some of that sort of Christianity here in Britain!" Not long after I spoke with him God took Eric to heaven, but his words have always lingered in my mind. "I feel I haven't begun to pray yet, Melvin," he told me. "You must get Britain on its knees!" That was his challenge to me, and I've been trying to do just that ever since.

I have been a student in the School of Prayer ever since I found Christ in 1955. I have not graduated yet – I'm still learning. I have been well tutored over the years. I was taught and encouraged to pray as a teenager in the Salvation Army, as a student at the Camberwell International Bible College, and as a young evangelist in Newcastle upon Tyne and Lincolnshire. I now see that throughout my Christian life God has been training me in intercession *for this hour of revival which has now come.* Now I pray more than ever before. Indeed, I could not continue without that sweet communion with my God. Each morning when I pray I feel a sacred freshness from God which gives me new strength to face the challenges of an exhausting ministry.

Prayer has been the key to every revival in the history of Christianity. Before the Day of Pentecost the apostles "all joined together constantly in prayer" (Acts 1:14). It was said of the Puritans of the sixteenth century, "They do meet in holy prayer four times a day." No wonder they took over the country in the next century!

Martin Luther was not satisfied with the religion into which he was born. His deep need for personal piety caused him to spend much time in prayer while he was the Professor of Theology at the University of Wittenberg. During the winter of 1512 he locked himself in a room within the tower of the Black Monastery at Wittenberg and prayed over what he was discovering in the

Scriptures. The Reformation was born through that time of prayer and study.

In Los Angeles in 1905 some Christians fasted and prayed together for revival, and the Holy Spirit fell on them as He had fallen on the apostles in Acts chapter 2. This was the beginning of the Pentecostal revival which has spread throughout the world.

The leaders of past revivals were shining examples of prayerfulness. David Matthews, an observer of the Welsh Revival, said Evan Roberts "had an experience which I believe was never repeated. Prayer was the keynote of his tireless life. No action taken or engagement entered into was done so without definitely committing the matter to God. His soul appeared to be saturated through and through with the spirit of prayer. It was the atmosphere in which he moved and lived . . . whenever one looked on his face, he seemed engaged in intercession."

Charles Finney wrote, "unless I experience prayer, I can do nothing . . . if for an hour I lose the spirit of grace and supplication, I am unable to preach with power and efficiency." Whenever Finney travelled he brought a "pray-er" with him – namely a certain minister named Nash. Often Nash wasn't even at the meetings but was in the woods praying! Small wonder that Finney's preaching got such wonderful results.

The rest of this chapter lists some of the important lessons about prayer which are being learned in the present revival in the UK.

Stirred in our hearts

First, in order to be able to pray for revival *we need to be stirred in our hearts*. We need to pray the sort of prayer which Jeremiah prayed: "Oh, my anguish, my anguish! I writhe in pain. Oh, the agony of my heart! My heart pounds within me, I cannot keep silent" (Jeremiah 4:19). He was so distressed about the state of his nation that it actually caused him physical pain. Prayer is not really prayer unless it is prayer for something which is longed for by the heart. Persistence in prayer is born out of a heart-longing rather than mental discipline, and persistence generally wins the day.

Listen to God

Secondly, we need to *listen to God*. I believe God is sending this new visitation because He has found an army of people who are willing to listen to Him. If we listen to God, we will know what He is doing. We will not be caught unawares when He acts. "Surely the Sovereign Lord does nothing without revealing his plan to his servants the prophets" (Amos 3:7).

In order to be able to listen to God, we need to meet with Him in silence and solitude. We gain security, confidence, power and peace from God only in silence. We twentieth-century workaholics need to turn away from the chafing pressure, mad scrambling and panting feverishness which we experience daily in our lives.

Luke tells us that "Jesus often withdrew to lonely places and prayed" (Luke 5:16). As a result He always had a restful, calm spirit, whether handling great crowds of people or teaching His disciples in private or taking them through a furious storm at sea or encountering a madman or raising the dead or healing multitudes of sick folk or meeting his critics face to face. He went on and on with unbroken calm amidst toil, suffering and misunderstanding. He was never anxious or hurried. His wonderful stillness is one of the greatest gifts He has given us. All the outstanding men of God in the past were people who listened to the Almighty in stillness and solitude.

Before I lead a service I spend some time praying alone in a quiet room. I give strict instructions that no one is to disturb me. I make myself still before God. Often He speaks to me with power during those times. I feel Him near, and sometimes it's almost as if He's standing next to me.

Get away from the noise, bustle and crowds which fragment your mind. Go into a quiet place. Do not talk. Keep your body still. Listen to God. In the stillness think of Jesus. Fill your mind with the Living Christ. Pause a while and let your soul catch up with you. Your life is enriched in the quiet place. You become easier to work with and a blessing to live with. So sit in God's presence. Let Him flood your heart. These times of silence are not apathetic escapism or a delusion. They are creative, dynamic and confidence-boosting.

Delightful prayer

Thirdly, where the revival is taking place *the whole tone of prayer has changed.* It is no longer a painful, tiresome chore; rather, it is a delight and a pleasure – it is exciting and powerful. It is no longer a dull monologue but rather a wonderful dialogue with our Maker!

Whenever prayer becomes a chore, then is the time to pray all the more. No man has so much need of prayer as the one who does not want to pray. Remember also that the great souls of the past who became mighty in prayer and rejoiced to spend three or four hours a day alone with God were once beginners. They went from strength to strength.

Prayer warriors

Fourthly, *we need to be prayer warriors.* We are engaged in a war, and we need to pray in a warlike way. We need to fight the forces of the enemy through prayer. In the Name of Jesus we have the power and authority to destroy them. And one of the secrets of successful spiritual warfare is getting up early in the morning to pray.

I know some Christians who are dedicated to this sort of prayer. If I happen to call on them early in the morning, I find that they are praying. If I phone them late at night they are praying then too! The ones who are winning the spiritual war are the ones who are getting up and praying while everyone else is still asleep. Sometimes they phone me or call on me early in the morning to get me to pray. Once I got back from a mission at 6.00 in the morning, having driven all night. I got into bed, but about half an hour later I was woken up by the "praying brigade"! Well, my flesh didn't appreciate it, but my soul did!

David was a man who knew the value of waking early to pray to God and to worship Him: "Awake, my soul! Awake, harp and lyre! I will awaken the dawn!" (Psalm 57:8). It is no wonder that God testified that David was a man after His own heart. God has promised that those who make it their habit to get up early to seek Him will find Him: "I love them that love me; and those that seek me early shall find me" (Proverbs 8:17, AV).

God guides us

Fifthly, we are discovering in this revival that *God guides His people through prayer*. God knows the beginning and the end of everything, so He is able to lead us to the right place at the right time. He wants to lead us at all times and to be in complete control of our lives.

I pray for guidance all the time in all sorts of places – whether I'm out jogging in the Wiltshire countryside or surrounded by 10,000 Zulus at a revival meeting in South Africa – whether I'm riding on a camel in the East or in an oxen cart in Malaysia or in the back of a pick-up truck in the heart of "Crocodile Dundee" territory in Australia. In a few minutes of communion with God, I know what He wants me to do in each situation. Because I have the mind of Christ I don't have to spend days judging a matter.

In the early morning our minds are fresh and unclouded by the conflicts of the day, so that is the best time to seek God's guidance.

The promises of God

Sixthly, *we must pray upon the basis of the promises of God*. The Word of God is full of precious promises. We need to believe them and apprehend them through prayer.

The great men of God in the Bible believed the promises which God made to them. Paul writes of Abraham: "he did not waver through unbelief regarding the promise of God, but was strengthened in his faith and gave glory to God, being fully persuaded that God had power to do what he had promised" (Romans 4:20-21).

Under the Old Covenant God proved faithful to His promises. Every time His people obeyed Him and fulfilled their side of the agreement, they saw the blessing and prosperity that He had promised. Under the New Covenant He is still the God of promise. Those who live by putting their faith in His words will see fulfilled in their lives all that He promises to do and give.

When you join a big corporation like IBM, ICI, Rank or BP, you are at a great advantage, because your firm's vast resources are at your disposal – there are great outlets for your creativity. It's just the same with the Kingdom of God, the greatest firm in the universe. Its powers and resources are inexhaustible, and they are ours to use. It is up to us to tap them, draw from them, channel them, live in them and claim all of them. *And we can do all that by prayer.* Jesus promised, "If you remain in me and my words remain in you, ask whatever you wish, and it will be given you" (John 15:7).

Pray with faith

Seventhly, *we must pray with faith.* When we pray, we must believe that our prayers will be answered. Jesus said, "Whatever you ask for in prayer, believe that you have received it, and it will be yours" (Mark 11:24). Pray that the mountain will move, believe that it will move – and move it will!

Faith and prayer are vital to eachother. We have to have them both in balance; one without the other is no good. A certain group of people in the Church today emphasize faith but give insufficient emphasis to prayer. This causes imbalance and disappointment in the lives of Christians.

They think that all they have to do is strain for faith without necessarily making any great effort in prayer. As a result they become sad, frustrated, empty and unrewarded.

On the other hand, if we pray without faith we are simply making sounds in the air. They never get further than the ceiling. The Bible says, "without faith it is impossible to please God, because anyone who comes to him must believe that he exists and that he rewards those who earnestly seek him" (Hebrews 11:6). In other words, when we come to God in prayer, we must come in an attitude of faith. God does not make faith optional – we must have faith if our prayers are to be heard by Him. He will not hear a prayer which is prayed in doubt.

There is no limit to what God can do for those who practise His laws of faith. But His blessing depends precisely on the degree to which you believe. Dr W. Sangster said, "Faith is like the sluice-gates on a canal or river. You move the great wheel and the gates move a little, and a small trickle of water seeps through. Turn the wheel full course and the flood gates open to their widest . . . and you have a flood of power and blessing."

Many Christians are brought up to believe that God wants them to have insurmountable problems and difficulties in their lives. But Jesus told us to move those mountains. It is easy to give in to a situation if you know in your heart that you do not have the faith to see the mountain moved. You are tempted to look for an excuse for it to stay. You may start saying things like "God is teaching me something through it" or "It is the cross I have to carry" or "There are others worse off than me". It is true that God teaches us through all the circumstances of our lives and that the mountains would not be there unless He allowed them to be. But His purpose is to bless us, not to make life unbearable for us. He wants us to have a faith that will move the mountains, not one which will leave them where they are! He wants to meet every need in our lives. Paul was not afraid to say to the Philippians, "my God will meet all your needs according to his glorious riches in Christ Jesus" (Philippians 4:19).

Jesus wants you to tell the mountain in your life to move, and He wants you to believe that it will do as you say (Mark 11:23). If you do these two things, the mountain really will move for you. Jesus did not say that you have to move the mountain yourself. God is the one who moves the mountain, not you.

Faith makes us kings in our lives. It throws light into the dark areas, it enables us to live in the fear of the Almighty and it puts fresh, invigourating energy into us. By faith and prayer combined we can possess the future, shake this nation and give hope to millions.

In the revival I am seeing people praying with faith in many places. They are asking big things of God and expecting Him to do them. God loves real faith like that!

Pray with humility

Eighthly, one of the hallmarks of the prayer in this revival is *humility*. Paul advised the Philippians, "in humility consider others better than youselves" (2:3), and that is an attitude which one can often see in revived churches. In Old Testament times the spiritual awakening under Josiah took place when the king gave the lead by abasing himself before God. Then God said, "Because your heart was responsive and you humbled yourself before God

. . . I have heard you, declares the Lord" (2 Chronicles 34:27). This has always been the pathway to revival blessing. When the people of God humble themselves in repentance, God always exalts them in revival. He has said, "I live in a high and holy place, but also with him who is contrite and lowly in spirit" (Isaiah 57:15).

Humility is the key to revival. "Humble yourselves, therefore, under God's mighty hand, that he may lift you up in due time" (1 Peter 5:6). Duncan Campbell, who was used so greatly during the revival in the Hebrides in 1951-52, said, "the key to God's supernatural visitation on these Islands was a spirit of exceeding deep humility, holiness, love and persistency in intercession."

Many of the afflictions we are called upon to endure, whether spiritual, mental of physical, are in fact the mighty hand of God upon us, bringing us low before Him. "Remember how the Lord your God led you all the way in the desert these forty years, to humble you and to test you in order to know what was in your heart, whether or not you would keep his commands" (Deuteronomy 8:2). Whether or not these wilderness experiences make us humble is up to us.

Jesus Himself set the example in humility: "being in very nature God, [He] did not consider equality with God something to be grasped, but made himself nothing, taking the very nature of a servant, being made in human likeness" (Philippians 2:6-7).

Pray in obedience

Ninthly, *our prayers must be accompanied by obedience.* Why should God answer our prayers if we are disobedient?

The words of Samuel are a challenge to the people of God today: "commit yourselves to the Lord and serve him only, and he will deliver you out of the hand of the Philistines" (1 Samuel 7:3). Are we ready to obey?

God is a speaking God, but if we are to hear Him we must have the right attitude – that is, a willingness to obey. Why should God speak to someone who is unwilling to obey? If there is sin in our lives we must repent of it and get it under the blood of Christ. This wipes the slate clean and enables us to hear God's voice.

Pray with persistence

Tenthly, *we must pray with persistence*. The prayer battle has been intensive in some places where revival has come. There have been many all-night prayer meetings. Christians have struggled through the dark hours to bring the blessing down and have refused to accept a denial from God. We need to persist in prayer, saying daily, "I will not quit!" This is the hardest lesson we have to learn about prayer. If a prayer is unanswered, it is probably because it hasn't been prayed enough. We need to keep praying until we have the assurance in our hearts that God has heard us and the answer is on its way. We must stir ourselves to stick in there! Remember, "Passionate persistence without impertinence produces progress."

Isaiah wrote, "You who call on the Lord, give yourselves no rest, and give him no rest till he establishes Jerusalem and makes her the praise of the earth" (62:6-7). What a bold statement! And yet Isaiah was perfectly right to make it. We should give ourselves and God no rest until

He has heard us, until Jerusalem is clothed in her beautiful robes again and is like a burning, shining light. We should bombard heaven until the answers come!

We not only need to pray persistently – we need to live our whole lives in prayer. Paul said, "pray in the Spirit on all occasions" (Ephesians 6:18).

Just before he died in prison in China the saintly Watchman Nee wrote:

> Ask. Since God is always there in the unseen, there is no situation on this earth in which you and I are powerless to do anything. Whether shackled by foes, or hampered by circumstances, whether totally paralysed or walled up in solitary darkness, we can pray, we can appeal to him, we can ask, and we shall surely recieve. God will act if we but go on asking.

United prayer

Finally, *we must practise united prayer*. Earnest, harmonious prayer is vital. Jesus promised, "if two of you on earth agree about anything you ask for, it will be done for you by my Father in heaven. For where two or three come together in my name, there am I with them" (Matthew 18:19-20).

I notice that in many older evangelical churches, although the Sunday congregations are large, the prayer meetings are attended by a mere handful of people. I find that the same is true of some new charismatic churches. I recently heard of one which had 200 people at its Sunday morning service, but only three at its main mid-week prayer meeting. By contrast, in many of the churches which are involved in the present revival the prayer meetings are bigger than the Sunday services! As a result these fellowships are filled with fresh zeal and energy.

Compare the amount of time which Christians spend in committees with the time they spend in united prayer! In most churches a great deal of time is wasted on endless, needless organization which produces nothing. Hours, days and weeks are spent on agendas rather than on agonizing before the Saviour. Frequently my co-workers and I put aside everything else and spend time in united prayer for our nation. We unite in loving, selfless prayer for a people who were once noble, undaunted, hard-working, thrifty, kind, principled and just, but are now lost, following false gods, drugged by the world's false values and living for money, pleasure, sin, worldliness and permissiveness.

How sad that for many Christians the prayer meeting has become just a boring part of the church routine. Many prayers are directed not to God but to the human listeners. Some people pray in the same words every time and sound just like a tape recording. Some turn their prayers into advice to the pastor or criticism about the way the church is being run. It is time to bury that kind of meeting, which kills the effect of real prayer. We need honest, earnest, passionate prayer which tells God eveything which is in our hearts.

I see the Church as a praying body, an army of earnest beseechers pulling down strongholds, a militant force kicking down the gates of hell. Prayer is not just one of the elements of church life – it is its primary force. Just look at the power of the prayer meetings in the Book of Acts!

A professor was once climbing the Weisshorn with an experienced Swiss guide. When they reached the top the professor stood looking at the magnificent view. Suddenly the guide pulled him down. "Get down on your knees!" he said. "A wind is coming, and you will only be safe if you are on your knees!" We are on a precipice today, and the wind of God's revival is coming. We can only be safe if we are on our knees in united prayer.

In Kimberley, Nottinghamshire, Pastor Noel and Kathy Klemenski took over a truly rockbottom work which had been declining for fifty years, and have seen the Holy Ghost make it a champion of churches. The BBC has featured it, and miracle upon miracle streams from it. It is now into its third extension, the church doors are rarely closed, hundreds visit its lovely modern restaurant each week, and nearly every hour of the day and night someone is praying, witnessing, counselling. Now its congregation is looking forward, within the next few years, to having the largest church in the British Isles, seating five thousand people. I have, during five visits, seen its work, seen it become a strong community, active, progressive, with spiritual influence, conviction and care. It is filled with the dynamism of the Holy Spirit, moving a whole district.

CHAPTER 10

A Revival of Conviction and Repentance

It's never too soon to repent, but it could soon be too late.

(W. Fuller)

As I take part in missions across the country I am increasingly encountering a spirit of conviction of sin and repentance. People are turning their backs on sinful habits. Previously lukewarm, indifferent Christians are gaining a genuine love for the Lord. Occult books and objects and pornographic magazines are being thrown on bonfires. At many of the meetings which I have led recently people have broken down and wept under the Holy Spirit's conviction. Sometimes they have been so overwhelmed by an acute sense of sinfulness that they have got up and confessed their sins aloud. Some Christians have criticized this, but if it is God who is causing people to do it, who are we to argue?

In some of my crusades the agonized cries of repentance coming from the meetings are so loud that they are heard in the surrounding streets. A sense of awe descends on the area, and even unbelievers can feel that something remarkable is going on. In homes round about people suddenly begin to weep. The local folk, who have previously been indifferent or even hostile towards my co-workers and I, are now friendly and respectful – even fearful. The mission is now the talk of the town; in shops, factories, hospitals, homes, gardens, streets, offices, trains and buses people are talking about the power of God. Towns are being taken by storm – not by organized mass evangelism, but by the Spirit of God. When the fear of God comes to a district the result is astonishing.

In the conversion of the zealous Pharisee Saul of Tarsus "a light from heaven, brighter than the sun" (Acts 26:13) blazed around him, striking him down and reducing him to a state of conviction and repentance. In just the same way that Eternal Light, in days of revival, bursts upon the slumbering consciousness of mankind, and with the same result. When the Holy Spirit came on the disciples on the Day of Pentecost Peter preached to the crowd. As a result "they were cut to the heart and said to Peter and the other apostles, 'Brothers, what shall we do?'" (Acts 2:37). The conviction which the Holy Spirit brought to their hearts spread over the whole city, and "Everyone was filled with awe" (verse 43). In the same way people are today being seized by an overwhelming conviction of sin. As Psalm 64 says, "God will shoot them with arrows; suddenly they will be struck down" (verse 7). People today are experiencing the sort of conviction which the saintly Robert Chapman knew when he wrote these words:

In his spotless soul's distress
I perceive my guiltiness;
Oh, how vile my low estate,
Since my ransom was so great!

Isaiah had a vision of the holiness of God. "Woe to me!" he cried from his heart. "I am ruined! For I am a man of unclean lips, and I live among a people of unclean lips, and my eyes have seen the King, the Lord Almighty"

(Isaiah 6:5). When Job received a revelation of God in His holiness he cried out, "I despise myself and repent in dust and ashes" (Job 42:6), even though God had said of him, "There is no-one on earth like him; he is blameless and upright, a man who fears God and shuns evil" (1:8). There are many Isaiahs and Jobs in the present revival: they are perceiving their sin and repenting of it. Repentance and contrition are what God requires in order that He may send revival: "The sacrifices of God are a broken spirit; a broken and contrite heart, O God, you will not despise" (Psalm 51:17).

An embezzler repents

At a crowded meeting in South Wales the pastor asked me, "Can you talk with that lady over there?" He pointed to a woman who sat weeping, being counselled by a female member of the church. I replied that I normally didn't counsel women, and in any case, I preferred all counselling to be done by the local believers. But the pastor said the woman was under an extraordinary conviction and would speak to no one but the preacher. So reluctantly I gave in, on the condition that a church member sat in with me. So we went into the vestry and talked, and after several minutes of weeping the woman came out with her secret. She had been a Christian for some years, but had backslidden. Some time ago she had stolen £20,000 from the firm she worked for. They had never been able to find out who had done it. She had felt rather pleased with herself and had enjoyed a very comfortable lifestyle on her ill-gotten gains. But for some reason she had felt drawn to the meeting that night.

During it she had been convicted of her sin. She said, "It all came back to me – I felt awful, gripped by fear . . ." God's wonderful Spirit had broken her down and shown her the state she was really in. She had repented and now felt forgiven by God. But what should she do next? She was terribly anxious about it.

I knew exactly what she should do, and gently I shared this with her. She must own up to her employers and offer to pay back all the stolen money with interest. She should also tell them why she was confessing her crime. I realized what the cost to her would be – the terrible shame, the press reports, the ridicule her family would suffer, losing her job, having to face imprisonment. I promised her that my colleagues and I would go with her and explain the reason for her new attitude. She agreed to go through with it.

She confessed her guilt to the firm's Board of Directors. They were utterly astonished. "We would never have found out that it was you who did it," said one of them. "You could have got away with it. Why have you owned up?"

We explained that God had convicted her of her sin and had led her to confess it.

"God told you to confess it . . ." repeated the hard-headed executive, looking mystified. "Well, I never thought God did that sort of thing for us businessmen. He's saved us a fortune!"

The directors were deeply impressed and moved by this lady's honesty and courage, but they said justice still had to be done. They asked us to wait outside while they decided what they should do. Finally we were called back in and she stood before them, waiting with bated breath, fully expecting that she would have to go to jail. But she was prepared to face that in order to be at peace with God.

There was a tense silence. The Chairman fumbled with his papers, took off his spectacles and put them back on again. He seemed just as nervous as the lady who stood trembling before him.

"I don't quite know why we are doing this," he said, "but we are unanimous about it . . . You . . . You were a trusted employee, but you failed us badly – you robbed us. Normally we would not hesitate to put a matter such as this into our lawyers' hands . . . but . . . but circumstances are so strange . . . You were in a church meeting, you said, and God told you to own up, you said . . . Well, it's all very strange, I must say. But since you have been so sincere and honest, and you have offered to pay everything back with interest, we have decided that we will not prosecute or dismiss you. We will demote you and send you to another department, and see how you get on. It's extraordinary . . ." he said. "Someone higher than us must be controlling us."

So the lady went on her way, scarcely able to believe that things had really turned out so well. She paid back every penny with interest and kept her job. Today she lives with a pure, undefiled conscience. Her confession of her sin had a huge impact on many people, particularly on the directors of her firm. Her story is a great testimony to the mighty working of the Holy Spirit in our generation.

I can think of numerous similar true stories. In one Cumbrian town people were powerfully convicted of sin by the Holy Spirit and were moved to put right any financial irregularities in their lives, such as bad debts or deceitfulness or theft. The next day people flocked to the local post office to buy postal orders to send, with a letter of confession and apology, to those to whom they owed money. Very soon the post office sold right out of postal orders!

Recently in a church which is seeking God for revival a young man was restored from backsliding and was convicted of a sin he had committed years before. He had defrauded British Rail by travelling for some time with an invalid season ticket. He made the long journey to the railway station concerned and there he confessed before the station-master and his staff and paid every penny he owed. Yes, God may put tremendous pressure on us in order to make our lives conform to His holy will. Our willingness to go to any lengths to put things right is a proof of a truly broken and contrite heart. Individuals and churches who are unwilling to put things right with God and bring everything to the light will not receive revival.

Paul wrote, "When they measure themselves by themselves and compare themselves with themselves, they are not wise" (2 Corinthians 10:12). That is precisely what many Christians do: they assess themselves by their own standards, rather than by God's standards. We must instead face our sins honestly and see them in the light of God's Word; we must view them as He does and deal with them before Him. Until we do, it is better that God should withhold the rain of revival, for it will do no good: "land that produces thorns and thistles is worthless and is in danger of being cursed. In the end it will be burned" (Hebrews 6:8). We must get rid of those thorns and thistles growing in unploughed ground. Hosea said, "break up your unploughed ground; for it is time to seek the Lord, until he comes and showers righteousness on you" (10:12). We must drive the plough through every obstruction; we must plough deeply so that the ground is mellow and soft, fit to receive God's seed and to bear fruit for Him.

Even ministers are repenting!

The current revival has had a striking impact upon some ministers. By God's supernatural power they have been deeply convicted of sin. They have confessed that they have done so little with the power and promises which God has put at their disposal, that they have compromized, that they have been lazy, that they have jealously criticized other ministers whom God has blessed and used powerfully. Their ministries have been transformed, and they have become active particpants in the revival. They have rededicated themselves to Jesus and now live only to serve Him in deep love. They have a new spiritual driving force in their lives. They are now men of prevailing prayer, bold preachers of the Word of God and compassionate shepherds of their flocks. Through their personal transformation their churches are being transformed, and thus the local community is feeling the impact.

Paul, writing to a young minister named Timothy, told him to "set an example for the believers in speech, in life, in love, in faith and in purity" (1 Timothy 4:12). It is so vital that Christian leaders are right with God. The words of this familiar hymn contain an important lesson for all ministers:

We cannot be channels of blessing
If our lives are not free from all sin.
We shall barriers be and a hindrance
To those we are trying to win.

Preachers need to put obeying God before pleasing men – otherwise their ministry will have no power. The fine

Pentecostal leader Robert Barrie wrote years ago: "The minister who is not delivered from bondage to public demands, who has linked his ministry with the desires and not the needs of his people, must inevitably abhor himself, eventually despise his ministry and become a miserable time-server living on his wits. This man cannot seek God for his ministry, for his message."

The quality of leadership in the revival is crucial. What matters is that preachers are anointed by God. They don't need to be posh, they don't need to have theology which is perfect down to the last tiniest detail. A certain revivalist preacher used to have a habit of putting his foot in it. In one of his sermons he told his listeners, "Moses got swallowed by the whale, and Jonah led the Israelites out to Nineveh"! But in spite of his mixed theology, many people were saved through his preaching that day.

The doctrine of sin

If we are to have revival, we must be prepared to tell people that they are sinners in need of God's forgiveness. In his *Studies in the Sermon on the Mount* Martyn Lloyd-Jones said:

> There is no true evangelism without the doctrine of sin, and without an understanding of what sin is. I do not want to be unfair, but I say that a gospel which merely says "Come to Jesus" and offers Him as a Friend, and offers a marvellous new life, without convicting of sin, is not New Testament Evangelism. The essence of evangelism is to start by preaching

> the law, and it is because the law has not been preached that we have had so much superficial evangelism . . . This means that we must explain that mankind is confronted by the holiness of God, by His demands, and also by the consequences of sin. It is the Son of God Himself who speaks about being cast into hell. If you do not like the doctrine of hell, you are just disagreeing with Jesus Christ. He, the Son of God, believed in hell; and it is in His exposure of the true nature of sin that He teaches that sin ultimately lands men in hell . . . It is only the man who is brought to see his guilt in this way who flees to Christ for deliverance and redemption.

Because man has grieved God by his sin there is a great gulf fixed between him and his Creator. However, many people do not even know that they are estranged from God. The great American poet Walt Whitman was once asked by his aunt, "Have you made your peace with God?" He replied, "I didn't even know we had a quarrel."

A cynic at an open air meeting once shouted to the preacher, "This Christianity of yours is just a crutch!" The preacher replied, "You're right – but who isn't limping?" Yes, the whole of mankind is limping because of sin. We are all crippled by its effects.

Charles Wesley said of sin:

> *Thou art darkness in my mind . . .*
> *Anger, lust and pride thou art.*
> *Thou art sin and sinfulness*
> *And unbelief of heart.*

People entertain wrong thoughts about sin. For

instance, we hear the sin of drunkenness referred to as just a disease, and we are told that homosexuality should be treated with kindness and compassion. But we must call sin *sin*. However much some camouflage it, it is still sin.

Once there was a queen who was quite mad. One day she escaped from the room in which she was being held. Her anxious attendants, knowing that she had a passion for roses, strewed thousands of them along the roads. Sure enough, the queen was drawn to the roses and was thus recaptured. In a similar way, the pleasures of sin have lured many people into captivity.

In Jonathan Swift's *Gulliver's Travels* Gulliver is shipwrecked on the island of Lilliput, which is inhabited by tiny people. While he is unconscious they tie him down with miniature ropes and pegs. When he awakes he finds that he is a helpless captive. Sin is like that – it binds us and makes us its prisoners. An unconverted person is a captive to the law of sin in his body and is impotent to deliver himself from this bondage.

There is a story of an Englishman living in Arabia who wanted to buy a house. He found one that was just right, so he went to the owner, who was an Arab, and asked him how much he wanted for it. The Arab asked an amazingly low price.

"But," said the Arab, "I don't want to part with the house completely, as I'm very attached to it. So can I knock just one nail in the inside wall, and that nail will be mine?"

The Englishman thought this must be to do with some Arab superstition. "Well, one nail can do no harm," he thought. So he agreed, and the contract was signed. However, when he saw the nail, he thought it was a rather large one. But he wanted the house, so he let the matter pass.

A few days later his wife told him, "The Arab came in today and hung a hat on that nail." Well, they couldn't say anything. The contract said it was the Arab's nail, to do with as he wished. But during the days that followed they were annoyed to find that there was a growing collection of items hanging on the nail.

One day, to their horror, the Arab came in with a dead donkey and hung that on the nail! The flies and the stench were so bad that they had to leave the house.

So to begin with sin is small and insignificant, but it grows until it pollutes everything.

A few years ago my family and I were on holiday in North Devon. My son wanted to play a game of golf, so we went to a nearby course – which happened to be a very posh, professional one. We paid our fee and got onto the course. Two hours later we spied an irate-looking man running across the green towards us. It was the Captain of the club. "You have sinned," he told us with some annoyance. "You have broken the club rules. Your first sin was that you tee'd off from the ladies' tee. Your second sin is that you only have one pair of clubs between you, and you should have a set each." So we were thrown off the course!

Before we left I said to the Captain, "I belong to the best club in the world. All its members have broken the rules and have admitted that they have broken them." "Which club are you referring to?" asked the puzzled Captain. "I'm talking about the Church of Jesus Christ!" I told him.

Unbelief in Christ

Unbelief in Christ is a sin – in fact it is the greatest sin which anyone can commit. But today's worldlings refuse to admit this. They argue that belief or unbelief in Christ is merely a matter of personal opinion. Men actually pride themselves on their unbelief, declaring with some brashness that they are "free thinkers".

Jesus Christ came into the world to save us from our sin. Refusal to believe in Him is really a way of saying that His Incarnation was not necessary – that sin is not a problem and that we do not need to be saved from it. This is an insult to God, for in effect it makes Him out to be a liar, for He has said that we do need to be saved from our sin. His Word says, "Anyone who does not believe God has made him out to be a liar, because he has not believed the testimony God has given about his Son. And this is the testimony: God has given us eternal life, and this life is in his Son" (1 John 5:10-11).

It is primarily the work of the Holy Spirit to convince men that refusing to believe in Christ is a sin. This is what our Lord said about the mission of the Holy Spirit: "When he comes, he will convict [or convince] the world of sin . . . because men do not believe in me" (John 16:8).

The coming judgement

People today don't believe in God's judgement, but they will have to face that judgement nevertheless. A young Christian was one day talking to an unbeliever and was trying to get him to come to church. The unbeliever, who happened to be a businessman, replied, "Church!

I don't go to church. I spend my time on Sundays settling my accounts." The Christian replied, "On Judgement Day God will settle His accounts with you!" This is a sobering truth. Jesus said, "whoever disowns me before men, I will disown him before my Father in heaven" (Matthew 10:33).

When you visit the supermarket you take a trolley and go around the aisles. You get bread, tomatoes, sugar, flour, cheese, jam, fruit – everything you need. The groceries just pile up in the trolley, and at this stage you don't have to pay for any of them. But finally you go to the checkout, and you cannot pass through until you have paid for everything. God's judgement works in a similar way. People may be erring, rebellious, worldly idol-worshippers, but often it appears that they get away with it. But finally they will all come to God's "checkout", and there they will have to pay for all their sin. They will pay by being shut out of heaven and suffering eternal damnation.

Many years ago an old soldier lay dying, and a minister came to see him. Sitting beside him he asked, "Are you afraid to die?" The old man answered in a weak and trembling voice, "No . . . I have fought many battles . . . I'm not afraid to fight this one." The minister was for a moment perplexed by this tough, soldierly reply. Then he asked: "But are you afraid to meet God?" The dying man said, "Now that's different . . . Yes, I am afraid to meet Him . . ." He was not afraid to die, but he was afraid to meet his Maker. All of us must eventually meet Him and face judgement. Romans 2:3 says, "do you think you will escape God's judgment?" Acts 17:31 says, "he has set a day when he will judge the world with justice by the man he has appointed". That Man is Jesus Christ:

"the Father . . . has given him authority to judge" (John 5:27).

It is not only the unsaved who will be judged, but Christians too. Charles Finney wrote: "A revival of religion is indispensable to avert the judgments of God from the Church . . . The fact is, Christians are more to blame for not being revived than sinners are for not being converted. And if Christians are not awakened, they may know assuredly that God will visit them with His judgments."

I often lose sleep because of the awful thought that millions are falling over the precipice and going down into hell, never having heard of the wonderful Lord Jesus who is able to save them. When God wakes you at night and shows you the state of our land, don't wait for the daylight to make things look less grim. Instead ask Him to keep that awful vision of the unsaved going to hell constant in your mind, and ask Him to give you the zeal to do something about it – to work for revival. For revival will rescue great numbers of people from the coming judgement, when all those who are unrepentant will be summoned to the feet of Christ.

Breakthrough in IRA territory

I went to a strongly Republican border area, which had never had a major crusade before. Three armoured police cars came when they heard of the crowds trying to get into the halls, thinking that it was a riot. The Holy Dove came down and miracles abounded. Two thirds of the families in the town came and we arranged extra services. A mighty revival!

CHAPTER 11

Aspects of the Revival

> The new revival . . . bursts the boundaries of traditional thinking.
>
> *(Alan Scotland)*

In this chapter we will be looking at some of the dominant characteristics of the revival which is presently sweeping through this country.

Supernatural power

The most obvious feature of the revival is a recovery of supernatural power in the Church. God is working in an amazing way, doing many miracles, healing countless sick people and setting many free from demonic oppression. In other chapters in this book you can read some true accounts of the working of God's supernatural power.

Sadly, for the most part the Church in the past has displayed very little of God's supernatural power. Tozer commented:

> If the Holy Spirit was withdrawn from the church today, 95% of churches would not miss him, they

would continue just as they have done for years, with the same programmes and formalities week by week . . . but if the Holy Spirit had left the early church, they would not have been able to function without him by at least 95%!

The cry of the atheist Ingersoll still rings out, challenging the sleepy Church in Britain today: "Show me the signs and wonders and miracles of the Bible and I will believe in Christianity." Edward England has written in *Renewal* magazine: "All our conferences, preaching and writing are of little value till we have demonstrations of God's power among the non-church community."

Few churches in the western world surprise anyone anymore. Still fewer astonish anyone. The Church is more pathetic than prophetic, more superficial than supernatural. It has become identified with prosperity, affluence and the natural. In Britain the membership of most evangelical and charismatic churches is drawn mostly from the middle and upper classes. Many of these Christians are Mrs Thatcher's and Mr Major's "babies" – affluent, wine-sipping yaks, or Mr Kinnock's "mice". They have neglected the poor, and the day of reckoning is coming. The good times are coming to an end for them. Only the supernatural Church – the miraculous Church of the Book of Acts – is going to survive with any credibility. Only the Bible-believing and -practising Holy Ghost churches will be triumphant; most of the rest will fade away, having to fight for mere survival.

Many renewed charismatic churches only went so far, and "used" the Holy Spirit to enlarge their memberships, increase their finances and prevent their people from going elsewhere. Ulterior motives have reigned for a generation, and now there are many charismatic groups and churches which have little supernatural power. They are becoming a mere shadow of the Church as we see it in the Acts of the Apostles.

In a certain Scottish church a new electric organ had been installed. One Sunday morning it broke down early in the service. Its power supply had failed. The congregation struggled on, singing without the music, while a couple of men set about fixing the organ. Just as the minister was about to lead the intercessions he was given a note which read, "The power will come on after the prayers." How apt! The power of God "comes on" after we pray. Prayer is essential before we see God move in further supernatural power.

Dreams and visions

Another feature of the revival is the dreams and visions which God is giving to His people. For years I was very cautious about such experiences. But in the revival in the UK these things are happening with such frequency that I have revized my attitude, and I now take them much more seriously. In many places which the revival has touched Christians have experienced the "Light Miracle". There are quite a few examples of this in the Bible: "An angel of the Lord appeared to them [the shepherds at Bethlehem] and the glory of the Lord shone around them, and they were terrified" (Luke 2:9); "As he [Saul, later Paul] neared Damascus on his journey, suddenly a light from heaven flashed around him" (Acts 9:3); "Suddenly an angel of the Lord appeared and a light shone in the cell. He struck Peter on the side and woke him up" (Acts 12:7). I know of many incidents in the revival today in which this Divine Light has been seen. People are seeing angels too. During one revival service a little child saw a white figure hovering in the air behind the preacher all through the meeting. She afterwards described the figure very clearly. "She has never seen anything strange before," her mother said, "and she hasn't heard about anything like this either, so I don't think she could have made it up." Months later the little girl was still talking about the wonderful sight she had seen. Many others too have heard the rumblings of heavenly chariot wheels.

At one revival meeting a beautiful aura – a sweet-smelling, out-of-this-world perfume – came down. Everyone in the meeting was drenched in it. The glory and splendour of God were almost tangibly present. Some of the people who had been to the meeting afterwards went to a cafe. The waitress, who had no idea where they had been, asked them, "What's that lovely perfume you're all wearing? It's heavenly!" Little did she know that it literally was a heavenly fragrance! Those who had been to the meeting still carried the perfume a whole day later.

In one Assemblies of God church scores were converted one night and great miracles of healing were seen. A "cloud" came down in one corner of the hall after the service. About twenty people all saw it at once. They fell on their knees in wonder and fear. This was a "glory cloud", the presence of God made visible. It remained for about twenty-five minutes and then gradually evaporated. It was an unforgettable moment in the history of that church!

A sense of God's awesomeness

Recently I had a very thrilling time of ministry in South Africa. In Capetown over 1,000 people were saved in just a few nights. They came from all sorts of ethnic backgrounds – black, white, Asian and mixed-race. People were touched by a sense of the awesomeness of God when we sang this song:

And when the sky was darkened in the void of the night,
He spoke into the darkness and created the light –
Our God is an awesome God.

Judgement and wrath He poured out on Sodom,
Mercy and grace He gave us at the Cross.
I hope that we have not too quickly forgotten that
Our God is an awesome God.

Our God is an awesome God –
He reigns from heaven above
With wisdom, power and love –
Our God is an awesome God.

It is terrible when a servant of God loses his sense of wonder and joy and becomes merely professional, or perhaps even bitter. As President Theodore Roosevelt said, "The poorest way to face life is with a sneer." Let us keep a sense of God's awesomeness and glory, a sense of wonder that we have been called to serve Him. Let us have hope and positiveness about our calling, so that we may in faith do great things for God, like Shakespeare's King Lear, who said, "I shall do great things . . . they shall be the wonder of the earth."

It is sad that so many people seem to miss the wonder in the world. They don't see God's glory in the creation, which is filled with such fascinating diversity. Einstein said, "He who can no longer wonder and stand in rapt awe is as good as dead." When he was a young boy James Watt sat fascinated as the boiling water in his mother's kettle kept lifting its lid up, and from his childish fascination the miracle of steam locomotion was eventually born. What great things can be achieved through our sense of wonder! A poet expressed the wonder of the constantly changing natural world in these words:

Yesterday the twig was brown and bare;
Today the glint of green is there.
Tomorrow there will be leaflets spare:
I wonder what will next be there.

The Christian faith is full of wonder. If a believer loses it, he is in a sad state. Saint Francis walked around starry eyed all his days and lifted great multitudes of the poor to faith in Jesus. He saw wonder as a gift of God. Many missionaries, working perhaps in the New Guinea Highlands or in the Amazon Basin, have been carried forward in their work by their Christian joy; they lived in awe of God, filled with love and gripped by a sense of wonder. Jesus' disciples had that sense of wonder. They were filled with "joy and amazement" when they met the resurrected Christ (Luke 24:41).

I was once chatting with two of my neighbours. One of them was talking about her son, who had left school a few months before. "He's got a job at the printing works," she said with maternal pride, "and they seem to like him very much. But, of course, he's always been such a nice boy, though I say it myself. He's so fond of his job that he often gets to work before time. He had only half an hour for dinner last Thursday – there was something wrong with one of the machines, and he went back early because he wanted to see them take it to pieces and mend it. He's awfully keen!"

The other neighbour nodded his head and laughed mockingly. "He'll soon learn that it doesn't pay to make a fool of yourself like that!" he said. I felt sorry for that disillusioned middle-aged man.

Life's difficulties need not rob us of our sense of joy and wonder if we keep our eyes on Jesus. Matthew Bridges experienced much sorrow in his life, and yet he gave us one of the most joyful and victorious hymns ever written:

Crown Him with many crowns,
The Lamb upon His throne;
Hark, how the heavenly anthem drowns
All music but its own!

A thousand or so years ago a Saxon evangelist named Brendan was trying to win the King of Wessex to Christ. The king asked, "What will I get out of it if I become a Christian?" Brendan replied, "O King, you will receive wonder upon wonder!"

Recently in my church we sang the hymn by John Greenleaf Whittier which contains the words, "I know not what the future hath of marvel or surprise". What a wonderful philosophy of life that is! So often, when we contemplate the future, it is with a certain amount of foreboding. We dread what the days ahead may bring us. No so Whittier. He looked ahead expecting marvel, surprise, wonder and miracle. That kind of outlook is being restored in the revival right now. People are beginning to expect God to do amazing things.

Closely connected with a sense of God's awesomeness is a holy, reverent fear of Him. Fear of God is the missing element in so much of contemporary Christianity. No amount of singing, worshipping, handclapping, dancing or celebration can make up for this lack; Bible weeks, campaigns, organizations and big personalities are no substitute for the fear of God.

The Bible is full of references to the fear of God. Solomon said, "The fear of the Lord is the beginning of knowledge" (Proverbs 1:7). Job said, "The fear of the Lord – that is wisdom" (Job 28:28). The psalmist said, "Let all the earth fear the Lord; let all the people of the world revere him" (Psalm 33:8).

Tozer said, "nothing deforms and twists the soul more than a low or unworthy conception of God". Moreover, nothing heals and uplifts the soul more than having a right conception of God and gazing upon Him. It is wonderful to stand with an awe-filled heart in the presence of the Almighty God. "And we, who with unveiled faces all reflect the Lord's glory, are being transformed into his likeness with ever-increasing glory, which comes from the Lord, who is the Spirit" (2 Corinthians 3:18). As we gaze upon the Lord the drabness, staleness, dullness and grubbiness of our carnal living vanishes, and freshness and vitality are ours.

In the revival which is now happening in this country I find this sense of the awesomeness of God time and time again. There is a wonderful, indescribable atmosphere in the revival meetings and services. You can feel the glorious presence of God, and you can see His wonderful power at work, converting, healing and delivering people.

A local revival

Evangelistic efforts in recent years have been highly efficient and well organized, but they have not been enough: they have not stopped the ceaseless downward trend of the nation. Nationwide missions have not brought revival. Of course, the Church should always be engaged in mission, but mission itself is not revival, as I have said elsewhere in this book. Something more consistent, urgent and local is needed. As the Archbishop of Canterbury recently said, "Evangelism, to be successful, must be local." What we need is revival on the streets, in the housing estates, in the huge inner-city tenement blocks, in the suburbs, in the villages, at the seaside. What we need is breakthrough at a local level. We need not method but marvels; not organizing but agonizing; not one big effort, but continuous power, love, communication and transformation. And this sort of local revival is precisely what we are beginning to see now in widely scattered parts of the UK.

In some places the revival is changing the local moral climate. It is lifting people up to the level of God's moral standards and commandments. Recently I had a phone call from the pastor of a church where I had led a crusade a few months before. He was bubbling over with enthusiasm, because since the crusade his church had grown by leaps and bounds. But he said the revival was also causing a problem, and that was the number of marriages he was now having to conduct! A lot of couples who had been living together had been converted in the mission and now wanted to do the right thing!

Often the side-effects of the revival glorify God in the local community. In places where the revival has come many crippled people have regained the use of their legs. Swollen, disabled feet have been reduced to their normal, healthy size and shape, and as a result people have had to buy new shoes to fit their new feet. In some places so many folk have discarded their old shoes that there has been a rush to the local shoe shops! One manageress commented that she hoped the revival would continue, since it was good for trade!

A passion for soul-winning

God is awakening in many Christians the desire to convert the lost people around them. Bob Geldoff inspired millions to give to the victims of the Ethiopian famine with the rallying cry, "People are dying – what are you doing to help?" We Christians can spiritualize his words: "People's souls are dying – what are we doing to help?" Today God is making many Christians aware of the need to evangelize the lost and is giving them the zeal to go out and do it.

By and large the Church in Britain long ago lost its passion for winning souls. Evangelism has been one of the Church's lost talents. Churches have been bogged down in social programmes, a parochial outlook, a concern for their own members. Most have been more interested in the monthly deacons' or PCC meeting than in evangelism; they have cared more about the monthly church finances than the monthly conversion figures!

"Restoration" was a favourite word among Christians in the 1980s. Many good things happened in this movement in the Church – there was a healthy emphasis on worship, praise, church structure, dealing with people's personal problems and taking care of the "sheep" (although some alarming mistakes were made in that area). But there was no restoration of the passion for winning souls. One of the outstanding features of the present revival is the recovery of that passion.

I know two young men named Roland and Bob who live in the city of Gloucester. Every weekday without fail they spend their lunch hours in the city centre speaking about Christ to the crowds of shoppers. They spend their Saturdays in the same way. Gangs of tough youths, instead of mocking them, listen to them with quiet respect. Many young folk have been delivered from drugs, drink and the occult through Roland's work. They have had a tremendous impact on the city centre. God is raising up people like them all over the country.

The revival is bypassing the established churches

Lewis Carroll's Alice is at one point wondering which direction she should go in. The rabbit asks her, "Which way do you want to go?" Alice replies, "Well, anywhere will do." The despairing rabbit says, "If you want to go anywhere, it doesn't matter what road you take." This is an apt description of the British Church in the latter part of the twentieth century. It has gone anywhere and everywhere *except the right way*. It has lost direction altogether. It is a case of the blind leading the blind. What an apalling witness the Church is to the world! Even the new evangelically flavoured Archbishop of Canterbury will not be able to make things right, because the Church of England is so monstrously sick and out of shape.

Recently I was leading a team of about forty young Christians in a Gospel campaign on the streets of Truro, the capital of Cornwall. We held some crowded meetings outside the Cathedral. We were not on church property and we had the permission of the local authorities to hold the meetings, but nevertheless during one of them an irate clergyman ran out of the Cathedral to complain about what we were doing. He pointed to the large banner which was being held aloft. "Take that banner down!" he demanded angrily. "People might think it is linked with the Cathedral!" And what were the offending words on the banner which the Cathedral staff hated so much? It read in big, bold letters, "JESUS IS LORD"! This incident paints a vivid picture of the worldly state of the Church of England today. Some of its clergy are actually offended by the Cross and the lordship of Christ!

So it is not surprising that the present revival is for the most part happening outside of the established denominations. Within them there are just a few bright spots of blessing amidst all the darkness, weakness and corruption.

Those Christians who have forgotten the unsaved masses who live in captivity are being passed over, while God is working through the loving few who are prepared to fully obey. This polarization will continue. Only those who are going all the way, who seem extremists in the eyes of the contemporary Church, will get the coming flows of God. This sustained outpouring is doing and will continue to do irreparable damage to the traditional church structures. This visitation of God is spelling great change for the Church. Those who are unwilling to follow will be left behind – far behind! As Archbishop Carey declared recently "the established churches are light years away from ordinary people".

Growing churches

However, we are seeing some remarkable church growth in some parts of the country. For example, when I first preached in Cornwall eighteen years ago there were only two or three little Pentecostal churches in the whole county. Few strong evangelical fellowships existed, and many of the chapels were empty or even closed. There was only a little renewal work going on and few healing missions were ever held. Mission had not been seen on a large scale for many years. Today there are at least twenty Pentecostal churches in the county, and contain as many as 1,000 new believers. Also some Baptist, Methodist, Anglican and Free churches have been touched by renewal. On a "local" level the fire of God is burning in places.

Sanctified believers

Today we are seeing a greater sanctification among believers. Touched by the Spirit of God, they are becoming more Christlike, and so as a result they are more effective witnesses for Him. As Bishop J. C. Ryle declared, "Unfailing courtesy, kindness and consideration are some of the greatest ornaments to the character of the child of God. The world can understand these things if it cannot understand doctrine." Someone once said, "The greatest need today is not for more Christian people, but for people who are more Christian."

Jesus is big news!

We are making the Good News news for today's people! As great miracles happen Jesus is becoming front page news in papers all over the country. A schoolboy once said, "How can you call something which is 2,000 years old news? Jesus is history, not news." But that boy was wrong – so wrong! When we preach the Gospel we don't just talk about what Jesus did when He was in the flesh – we talk about what He is doing today. He is still active! He is still making news today, just as He did in New Testament times – 2,000 years are nothing to Him! The sun is almost unimaginably old, but it is still active, still sustaining life on earth. The Son of God, who created the sun and the earth, is still active too. The Gospel still works – this modern revival is proving it in these islands today. Powerful words, works, wonders are the order of the day!

A team effort

An important aspect of the revival is that it is a team effort: whole congregations are working for it, not just ministers and evangelists. Someone once likened the Church in the West to a football match. In the stadium are tens of thousands of people, badly in need of exercise, watching twenty-two exhausted men who badly need a rest. It has been the case in the Church that most people have sat by watching and criticizing while a tiny few have done all the work and achieved all the results. The revival is changing this sad state of affairs.

The traditional type of church is like an old-fashioned fighter aeroplane. It is a solo flight – one man (the minister) is the navigator, the gunner and the pilot. But the new, revived body of Christ is like a jumbo jet – it is packed with all sorts of people with different gifts, characters and backgrounds, all working, worshipping and rising together in the mighty, powerful aircraft, reaching new heights for God. Slowly but gradually (although still in a minority of fellowships) the biblical concept is returning.

Baptism in the Spirit

In all my crusades I pray for people to be baptized in the Holy Spirit. I am not ashamed of this mighty blessing – I don't keep it dark until people can understand it. It is an integral part of the Gospel. In his first sermon the Apostle Peter preached the whole Gospel – including the baptism in the Holy Spirit – and I follow his example.

A rebirth of faith

Another prominent feature of the revival is the growth of faith among believers. Many of God's people are realizing that faith, coupled with humility, is the mightiest power in the universe and that God has given this power to them.

We are seeing a rebirth of faith, as Christians gain a new supernatural confidence. They are recognizing that the biggest task which any believer has is to become a giant of faith, like Elisha, Elijah, Gideon, Moses, Paul and Peter. Today many children of God are hearing the call to faith after decades of spiritual coldness.

God will do anything for the man or woman of faith. For the Christian who has faith God will move heaven and earth and make the sun stand still; for faith He will move mountains, He will make iron float, He will make rivers flow backwards. God is today doing the impossible for His children of faith. This is perhaps the greatest rediscovery which the revival has brought to us. We are stretching our faith to believe that God will do something far greater than anything we have ever seen before!

Starting with the individual

This is a revival which starts with the individual believer and then reaches out to the uttermost parts of the earth. Revival always begins at the personal level; it is always a clean-up and a clear-out! If our ways are offensive to God there is no way we can expect His blessing. Revival will elude us. We need to learn God's ways, to find out from His Word what He is like – and then we must choose to imitate Him. As we do so, we will find ourselves being revived. The Word says, "Come near to God and he will come near to you" (James 4:8). But many Christians expect Him to come near while they remain far away from Him in conscious disobedience. But He won't come near under those conditions. *We* have to make the first move; just as with slimming, nobody else can do it for you!

A divine pattern

Those of us who are involved in the present revival are learning from God and beginning to see a divine pattern emerge:

1. God does not need large numbers to do His work or launch His invasions. He only needs a faithful few in each place – surrendered, willing, sacrificial and given up to him. He does not see the empty seats in the services. He sees the men and women who do come to church, who are willing to serve Him, who have hungry, open hearts. He wants prayerful, pure, loving people.
2. Every church, fellowship and house group is different. We must accept one another's different distinctives and the particular characteristics which God has given us. We must let the Holy Spirit do what He wants in each different situation – we must let Him control our churches and meetings. We must be open to Him. God keeps saying to us, "Don't judge yourselves against others. Don't copy – be yourselves in my Spirit. Don't worry about numbers – I'll find the people I want, wherever they are. Do what I tell you to do – do your part and I will do my part. I'll bring the people to you."

CHAPTER 12

Reaching Minority Groups

> I know your works . . . if God opens the door, no men can shut it.
>
> *(Revelation 3)*

One of the notable characteristics of this revival is the fact that the power of God is reaching minority social groups which are normally untouched by the churches.

A doorway into Islam

There has been a significant move of God amongst the Moslem people of east Birmingham. When some "Love Europe" teams went to the area for a month a couple of years ago, some of the people who preached Christ in the open-air meetings were pelted by Islamic fundamentalists. Recently I preached at a revival crusade in the district. The local pastors told me about the difficulty of getting the Moslem people to come to church. Opposite one Assemblies of God church a huge mosque is being built which will take 5,000 people at a time. One pastor told me that whenever he put up a poster saying "Jesus Christ is the Son of God" or something like it, it was always torn down within a few days.

However, the power of God is able to break down such

social and religious barriers. During the campaign huge numbers of Moslems attended the meetings. One Moslem man who was converted came to twelve services in a week, bringing along dozens of his family and friends. He put up our crusade posters all over the front windows of his shops. One Moslem eighteen year-old came to every one of the meetings and was born again. He was given a Bible to read, and his verdict was, "It's wonderful! It's better than the Koran." Now he and many other young Asians have joined local churches.

During the campaign I was invited to speak to some of the members of a mosque. Some of those who came to hear me were sick in body or in mind and had come hoping for healing. On the walls were pictures of the Ayatollah Khomeini. The Mullahs wore their distinctive hats, the other men wore skullcaps and the women wore veils over their faces. I told them that my God was the God of Abraham, Isaac and Jacob; I told them how the books written by Moses described God as "the Lord our righteousness" and "the Lord our healer". I recited the Ten Commandments to them. They murmured in agreement, some of them smiling. I could see that I was on the right wavelength. I told them about the great power of God, and how He had worked through Elijah and Elisha. Frequently my listeners would lift their hands and heads towards heaven and give a cry of agreement. They listened to me almost as if I were one of them.

Then they asked for prayer. One of the Mullahs explained that many of their people had spoken in glowing terms of the love which had been shown towards them at the revival meetings. They had witnessed the power of prayer; many lives had been changed and many people had been released from pain and paralysis. I then gently explained to them about the One who had done all these miracles – the Lord Jesus Christ. We had prayed in His name, and He had answered. My listeners had great respect for Him. I had to choose my words very carefully now, but these people were willing to listen to the Gospel. Then we prayed together in the Name of Jesus. God had opened a door into the very territory of Islam.

A remarkable awakening has come to the Moslems of east Birmingham, and the work still continues. Only the hand of Christ can open up hearts and minds which are closed; it is a miracle of God. As John said, He "holds the key . . . What he opens, no-one can shut" (Revelation 3:7).

Hell's Angels become God's Angels

Another fringe social group which has been touched by the present revival is the Bikers. There are about 30,000 of them in the UK. They are an unmistakable and rather intimidating sight, with their leather jackets, ragged denims, beards and helmets. Some of them are in their early teens, others are in their twenties or thirties. Living with their girlfriends, drugs, alcohol and violence are often all elements of their wild, amoral lifestyle. They are frequently in conflict with the police. Some of them are mixed up with the occult and the New Age Movement. Never before have these people been seriously touched by the Gospel, but today there is an amazing moral and spiritual revival going on amongst them.

A while ago I was taking part in a divine healing service at a Pentecostal church. I was just about to stand up to preach, when we heard a huge roaring noise coming from outside the church building. I thought it was just some noisy youths passing through, since the church was on a busy main road. But in fact it was about fifty Bikers turning up to attend the service.

Unaware of what was about to happen, I got up on to the platform, and the pastor introduced me to the congregation. Then the doors at the end of the church crashed open loudly, and a small army of leather-clad young men marched in. The stewards didn't know what to do, and the Bikers just swept past them and made for the empty seats. One after another they trooped in, the door swinging back and forth. There seemed no end to them! Some of them were very big, muscular men. Most had beards, and many were carrying their helmets. On their jackets were swastikas and the name "Hell's Angels". Some of them had bands tied around their foreheads. They filled every available seat, and some of them had to stand.

The pastor wiped his brow nervously and said, "We've got trouble here, I think. What do you think we should do?"

"Get them converted," I replied.

I preached a sharp Gospel message about sin, repentance and forgiveness; I told them they had to change their whole way of life, by God's mercy and grace. The Bikers listened intently all the way through. When I appealed for those who wanted to become Christians to come forward, the Bikers were on their feet before anyone else. They rose like one man and rushed down the aisles. The pastor, closing his eyes with fright, whispered, "This is it!" They stopped at the pulpit, their hands reaching out penitently! These big, tough men – their swastikas shining under the overhead lighting –

were weeping, tears dropping from their beards. Some of them cried loudly as I led them in a simple, sincere, heart-rending prayer. "Lord, Lord, forgive me!" they prayed, some of them almost shouting. The place was flooded with the supernatural power of God. What a night!

The local Christians were surprised by all this, to say the least. Some of them thought this mass conversion would be just a seven-day wonder. But in fact there was a lasting change in these Bikers' lives. And gradually some of their women were won over as well. The work amongst the Bikers has grown since then, and there are now between three and five hundred fully discipled Bikers in the UK. They are truly saved and sanctified; they have been baptized and they are now following the Lord. Bridgewater in the West Country and Wokingham in Berkshire have seen the Bikers touched in a powerful way, but encouraging things are happening in other parts of the country too. Some Bikers are now working among their fellows as full-time evangelists.

There has been a striking moral revival amongst the Bikers who have been converted to Christ. When they become Christians they either part with their women or marry them. They are also learning to obey the law – breaking it used to be one of their pastimes! They are learning to have consideration for others, and they no longer rev their machines near people's homes late at night. On their backs and bikes the name "Hell's Angels" has been crossed out and replaced by "God's Angels". Now they roar up the motorways at the top (legal) speed with texts like "Prepare to meet thy God" and "Where will you spend eternity?" written on their bikes. But they still have long hair – even the evangelists!

They hold Bikers' Rallies, where they hear the Word preached and worship God with great enthusiasm, singing loud choruses, dancing before the Lord, clapping and shouting the name of Jesus until they are hoarse. The police come to keep an eye on things, but there is nothing for them to do. There is no fighting, drug-taking or immorality – only Christian joy. They used to swear at the police and fight them, but now they give them cups of tea and Gospel tracts and tell them about Jesus, to the amazement of the bobbies!

However, it is proving to be difficult for them to become integrated into the life of the mainstream churches. Some converted Bikers once went to an Anglican parish church. They advanced down the aisles, smiling at the vicar. There were about forty of them. They were wearing black leathers and had chains on their arms and heavy boots on their feet. The vicar walked nervously down to them. "What d-do you w-want?" he asked. The leader of the Bikers replied, "We've come to do our stuff!" – meaning they had come to worship God. But the vicar clearly thought he meant they were going to smash the place up!

Even some evangelical churches have not welcomed them for long. It seems that their loud, exuberant worship is too much for some rather sedate Christians. They have asked me for advice many times about the increasing problem of their relationship with the established churches. The Church just isn't ready for this Biker revival – it wasn't ready for many of the great awakenings of the past. I have advised the Christian Bikers to start their own churches and fellowships, where they can worship freely within their own culture. I thank God that such churches are now in existence and growing.

CHAPTER 13

The Glory is Coming Down

And the glory of the Lord will be revealed, and all mankind together will see it.

(Isaiah 40:5)

Giving glory to God

The highest and most sacred purpose of revival is that God should be glorified. Arthur Wallis said, "You cannot adequately explain revival, but it is a deep penetration of His glory." The revival which is now happening is a manifestation of God's glory. Isaiah wrote, "the glory of the Lord will be revealed, and all mankind together will see it" (Isaiah 40:5). Anyone who catches a glimpse of that effulgent glory (and one glimpse is enough to spoil him for all the earth) will go forth, whatever the cost, to spread the Good News.

In our revival meetings we make much of the glory of God. We sing:

It's coming down, down, down,
It's coming down,
Oh the glory of the Lord is coming down!
When the saints begin to pray

The Lord will have His way,
And the glory of the Lord,
It's coming down!

Mikhail Gorbachev once visited a certain city in Russia. Normally a Soviet premier would see only Communist Party leaders, but Gorbachev, the instigator of the policy of *glasnost*, had asked to see leaders from other sections of the community as well. He shook hands with people from various ethnic groups and with the leaders of the local churches. He asked the leader of the Pentecostalists what his message was. The minister, wishing to play it safe, replied, "Peace on earth and good will to men." Gorbachev said, "But don't forget the rest, will you – 'and glory to God in the highest'!" If even a Communist leader can speak of God's glory, the people of God must not be slow to glorify Him. David said, "Ascribe to the Lord the glory due to his name; worship the Lord in the splendour of his holiness" (Psalm 29:2).

A victory is only complete, a healing or miracle is only finalized when we give God all the praise for it. Kathryn Kuhlman used to pray before her great healing meetings in Los Angeles, "I will give you all the glory for this night . . . I give you all the praise . . . You will be glorified, precious, lovely Jesus." Her prayer was full of glorification to God.

We often read in the Gospels that Jesus' miracles caused men to praise God. In Luke 13 we read that He laid His hands on a crippled woman, "and immediately she straightened up and praised God" (verse 13). In Matthew 9 we read that Jesus healed a paralytic. "When the crowd saw this, they were filled with awe; and they praised God" (verse 8). When God is glorified, it spreads like a fire.

To remember to constantly glorify God is the pathway to a blessed, rich life. Here is a scripture we would all do well to pray and say every day: "to the only God our Saviour be glory, majesty, power and authority, through Jesus Christ our Lord, before all ages, now and for ever more!" (Jude 25).

You see, when you are in love, you don't spend all day dawdling in front of the mirror admiring yourself – you spend your time looking at your beloved, giving him or her your admiration, your time, your attention, your love and your praise. If we truly love God this will be our attitude towards Him. We will want to give Him all the praise and glory.

The glory of God should be the motivation behind everything we do. When we become aware of any other motivation, let us avail ourselves of the cleansing blood of Christ through confession, and let us look to God in faith, trusting that by His Spirit He will "take captive every thought to make it obedient to Christ" (2 Corinthians 10:5).

Glorifying ourselves

The spirit of our age encourages people to glorify themselves. Mohammed Ali used to say, "I am the greatest!" At the funeral of one of the infamous Great Train Robbers there were no hymns – just a tape recording of Frank Sinatra singing "I Did It My Way". Arrogance to the very end! This egotistical attitude has permeated the Church. John Stott has written, "Personal vanity lies at the root of many church divisions." Jesus told us, "whoever wants to become great among you must be your servant" (Matthew 20:26). We must yield to God and to other people; we must give the glory away, we must not take the credit. God is looking for people who are unsullied and unaffected by their success.

In this "He-Man" age – this era of Superman, Terminator II, the Incredible Hulk, Rambo and the A-Team – we are very much out of step with our society if we choose to take no glory, to be contrite, to humble ourselves. But God bids us to turn away from our self-conceit, to deflate the hot-air balloons of our egos, to give all the glory to Him.

Christians in leadership are particularly prone to a certain temptation – namely, to bathe in self-esteem and to take the credit that rightly belongs to God. Difficult though it may be for us to understand, it is a firm scriptural principle that God will not share His glory with anyone else. He has said, "For my own sake, for my own sake, I do this . . . I will not yield my glory to another" (Isaiah 48:11). Of course, if God uses you to bless people they will thank and praise you and will look up to you. It is vital that leaders don't let this go to their heads. If people give you thanks, try to pass on some of the thanks to some other person. As Paul said, "Let us have a willingness to let others have the credit" (Romans 12:10, J. B. Phillips). Here is a wise old saying: "There's nothing God cannot do if we keep our hands off the glory." The godly Oxfordshire evangelist Fred Smith said about glorifying God, "It is not denying the power you have, but admitting that the power comes *through you* and not *from you.*"

By stealing God's glory His people bring upon themselves spiritual impotence and defeat. Alan Richardson said, "Rebellion attributes to self the honour and glory due to God."

God gives us His glory

It is God's will that we should give Him glory, but there are occasions when *God gives His glory to us* in the sense that He manifests His presence in a tangible way. During Israel's wandering in the wilderness the *shekinah* glory of God was often seen: "the cloud covered the Tent of Meeting, and the glory of the Lord filled the taberbacle" (Exodus 40:34). The shepherds saw God's glory on the night of Jesus' birth. Peter and John saw Jesus glorifed on the Mount of Transfiguration. In the present revival people are having similar experiences of God's glory.

I was once preaching in a small chapel in Cornwall when the glory of God came down. When it came many people began to weep. I felt so weak at the knees that I could hardly stand up, and after delivering a short word I was swept off my feet along with everybody else by the magnificent power of God. We experiencd a heavenly, other-wordly radiance and joy. When we got to our feet again an hour later we were filled with the Holy Spirit. We sang and danced and then marched out into the surrounding country lanes. We proclaimed Christ to passers by, just as the apostles did at Pentecost. Nor did the glory die away overnight. Many of those who had experiencd this visitation of God accompanied my team and I as we went to preach in the next town. As a result the subsequent meetings were blessed with extraordinary power. The conversions, growth, changed lives, quality testimonies and new churches planted since in that area have been astonishing. Thousands gather nightly across the UK giving God glory, and seeing "no man, save Jesus only" (Matthew 17:8).

CHAPTER 14

The King is Coming!

It is later than you think.

(former President Reagan)

The Nicene Creed includes this affirmation: "He shall come again with glory." Our Saviour, the Lord Jesus Christ, is coming back to earth to establish His Kingdom. When the Archbishop of Canterbury crowns a monarch at Westminster Abbey he uses these thousand-year-old words: "I give thee this crown to wear, until He who reserves the right to wear it shall return." When King Jesus returns all other kings will bow the knee to Him.

A few years ago a missionary was in Amman, the capital of Jordan. There were barriers across the main road, so the traffic was completely snarled up – the streets were packed with stationary cars, lorries, bikes, carts and horses. Soldiers and policemen were everywhere, lining the streets and watching from the rooftops. The pavements were crammed with people, waiting expectantly. The missionary squeezed his way through the dense crowd and asked a policeman what the big hold-up was. "Don't you know?" he replied, looking at the visitor as if he were stupid. "The King is coming – and when the King comes everything must stop!"

The same will also be true when the King of Kings returns – everything will stop then. There will be one last revival in the world, through which the whole earth will be filled with the knowldge of the glory of God, and then King Jesus will come.

That final revival has already begun in Britain. Believers are repenting of their indifference to the honour of our holy God and the desperate need of the unsaved people around them; they are repenting of their unbelief and their self-seeking ambition; they are repenting too of the wickedness of this permissive, secular nation. This repentance is turning God's people into a militant force which will bring revival to every part of this land. Have *you* repented? Are *you* committed to revival? Are *you* seeking the Lord with all your heart on behalf of our nation?

The wrath of God has already been declared against this nation, and that wrath will surely come. And yet He will restrain His just anger in response to such repentance by His people. For a little while His mercy and grace are being revealed. There will be a last harvest, a final revival and turning to the Lord, commencing now. Then fire, judgement, retribution and hell will be the lot of all Christ-rejecting people.

The preaching of the message that the King is coming, and that people must get right with Him or face His judgement, is causing many thousands of unsaved folk to fear God. Convinced that the judgement of God is coming, they receive Jesus as their Saviour, turning away from their previous lives. They abandon the pubs, the discos, the gambling dens, the dirty videos; they reject worldliness, materialism, lustfulness and permissiveness and instead turn to the King of Kings and love, adore, worship, magnify and serve Him.

It is essential that at this hour the attention of God's people should be fixed on the fact that Jesus is coming back. Dr Steve Travis, Deputy Principal of St John's College in Nottingham has said, "Christians whose hope is fixed on Christ's coming will be people who are still growing – in love and wisdom, in their awareness of God and in the quality of their Christian obedience."

A theology teacher used to be fond of saying that Christians' knowing that Jesus is coming back should not mean that they are constantly asking, "When will the whistle blow for the end of the game?" Rather, they should be asking, "Where should I be now, to receive the next pass?" We must serve God as best we can while the "game" is still going on. Do you know where on the "pitch" God wants you to be in this final part of the "game"? Is your heart open to Him in this final outpouring of His grace before He comes again? Play your part in the great awakening that is now going on in Britain!

A consciousness of the imminence of Christ's return is a key feature of the present revival. This hope gives a new glow and excitement to Christians' faith, and the knowledge that they will soon meet their God gives them a renewed fear of Him, which causes them to live pure and holy lives. The coming of the Lord Jesus is much spoken about, sung about and prayed about among those caught up in the revival. It is common to hear believers saying to eachother things like "Will He come again today?" or "Jesus is coming soon!" or "The King is on His way!" When we say goodbye we often say, "See you tomorrow, if Jesus doesn't come before then!"

This is not a time for despondency. This present age will finish not with tragedy but with triumph for the Church. We are going to be the victors on the spiritual battlefield! This is not a time of dearth but a time of harvest. Let us be incorrigible optimists in the heat of the battle, for we know that the kingdom of this world will soon be the Kingdom of our God and of His Christ!

CHAPTER 15

The Cost of the Revival

> The greatness of a man's power is the measure of his surrender.
>
> *(William Booth)*

If you study the history of the revivals of the past you will find that in each case there was a price which had to be paid for such a move of the Holy Spirit. The cost of revivals is enormous. God demands absolutely everything from His people.

In order to bring the delivering grace of God to the multitudes who are in darkness we must be prepared to make sacrifices. In this new impetus of the Spirit there is much fasting, crying and praying, rather than dancing, frivolity and lightness; there is much faith, boldness and fighting for King Jesus rather than socializing, worldiness and drinking. It costs us personally to have a revival. You may lose some of your friends. They may want to have fun dancing and prophesying in a corner; they may not want to work hard. If you are prepared to believe, pray, submit, sacrifice, surreneder, obey – if you are ready to face persecutions, accusations, condemnations, criticisms and misunderstandings – then you will see results.

Some saints I know have given their last penny to promote the Gospel. Some have given up their time to fast and pray earnestly. One couple even put off their wedding day by six months so that they could spend more time evangelizing – a great sacrifice for young people to make. Some have cancelled their holidays to spend the time spreading the Gospel instead. Some have given up their jobs to work for Jesus full time, without a guaranteed income from any source. No wonder revival is breaking out among such folk!

Jesus made the supreme sacrifice and paid the maximum price to bring us victory. Was humanity poor? Jesus became as poor as the poorest. Were they despised? He was more despised than anyone. Were they friendless and alone? He kept a lonely vigil in the Garden of Gethsemane and the following day died in agony on the Cross. Were they filled with sin and burdened with disease? He bore their sins and sicknesses. Jesus paid the price, and we must too.

Some Christians are not prepared to pay the price of revival. Some start out working for revival enthusiastically, but eventually the glamour wears off and they decide that the price is too high. They drop out as some of Jesus' followers dropped out, murmuring to themselves, "This is a hard saying."

Are you ready to pay the price? Or are you slipping, lax and slothful, weak and cold in spirit? Are you ashamed to be fervent in your devotion to the Lord? Remember, you have been given salvation. "From everyone who has been given much, much will be demanded" (Luke 12:48).

I often say at my rallies, "You cannot stand in revival victory until you kneel down. You cannot get high with God until you get low before Him. You cannot reach the top with God's power unless you start at the bottom. You cannot scale the heights until you have clambered over the rocks."

Let us now look at the many different sacrifices being made by the people who are caught up in the present heaven-sent revival.

Self-death and obedience

I see a self-giving, obedient people being raised up across the nation – small in number, but dedicated and self-crucified for Christ. Obedience is the mark of every true follower of Christ. General Carpenter of the Salvation Army used to say, "The only way to the victorious Christian life is to say 'Yes' to Jesus and to keep on saying 'Yes'." Dr Sangster encouraged Christians to make Christ "the King, not the President, for a king rules for life".

Jesus said, "Come to me, all you who are weary and burdened, and I will give you rest. Take my yoke upon you and learn form me, for I am gentle and humble in heart, and you will find rest for your souls. For my yoke is easy and my burden is light" (Matthew 11:28-30). Here is the call to self-death. We must take the yoke of obedience upon us in order to find rest for our souls. Jesus demands submission: "If you love me, you will obey what I command" (John 14:15). To some people this sounds like slavery and a contradiction of Christ's offer of freedom. But freedom from sin and submission to Christ belong together. Each involves the other. "You have been set free from sin and have become slaves to righteousness" (Romans 6:18). In submission to Christ we find our only true freedom.

We are not being asked to submit to an ogre or a tyrant but to the Lord Jesus, who comes not to impoverish our lives but to enrich them. Why should we shrink from a total surrender of our lives to Him? He is "humble in heart". This humility was powerfully expressed by His stooping to wash His disciples' feet and by His dying to cleanse His people from their sins. He was humble enough to submit to His Father's will, and He asks us to do the same. Will you submit all of yourself to Him, so that revival might come to your family, church, community, city or county? In order that revival may come and stay in all its fullness Christ must be resurrected within us, and that can only happen if we die within. Jesus said, "unless an ear of wheat falls to the ground and dies, it remains a single seed. But if it dies, it produces many seeds" (John 12:24).

This self-dying must be a renunciation of ourselves, our abilities and our resources. We must come to the place of weakness and emptiness, so that His strength may be made perfect in us. We must live as branches of the True Vine, Jesus. The Vine has everything, the branches have nothing. He said, "no branch can bear fruit by itself; it must remain in the vine. Neither can you bear fruit unless you remain in me" (John 15:4). This fact, obvious to the mind, does not sink down easily into the heart. We have to learn the lesson through the bitter experience of failure.

This attitude of self-renunciation characterized the life of the Saviour. He said, "the Son can do nothing by himself; he can only do what he sees his Father doing" (John 5:19); "My teaching is not my own. It comes from him who sent me" (7:16); "I have not come on my own; but he sent me" (8:42). We are called to imitate this attitude: "any of you who does not give up everything he has cannot be my disciple" (Luke 14:33). Paul set forth the life of self-renunciation when he wrote, "I have been crucified with Christ and I no longer live, but Christ lives in me" (Galatians 2:20).

Part of this attitude of self-dying is a complete dedication to the will of the Father. We must say with Jesus, "My food is to do the will of him who sent me and to finish his work" (John 4:34).

James wrote, "Wash your hands, you sinners, and purify your hearts, you who are double-minded" (4:8) – or, as the Berkeley Version puts it, "you people of divided interests". Let your sole interest be serving Jesus! Do not let your heart and your commitment be divided. Do not be diverted, but instead give yourself to Him – die within and live only for Him!

Closely connected with self-dying is repentance. Charles Finney wrote, "A revival of religion may be expected when Christians begin to confess their sins one to another . . . where there is an ingenuous breaking down, and a pouring out of the heart in making confession of their sins, the floodgates will soon burst open, and salvation will flow over the place." The God who dwells in the "high and holy place" has promised "to revive the spirit of the lowly and to revive the heart of the contrite" (Isaiah 57:15). A spirit of contrition among the saints is therefore a strong indication that revival is coming.

A strong emphasis on the Cross is vital if we are to have revival. An old pioneer evangelist in the Salvation Army once said to me when I was a tiny lad, "The Cross is the attraction, my son. Go and preach it one day!" How right he was. The Cross is indeed the attraction – every revival is a return to it. And his words to me were a true prophecy, for since the age of seventeen I have indeed preached the Cross.

Many doors are made up of four panels with a cross in between them. It was the carpenters' guilds of the Middle Ages who invented this design. Their motto was

Jesus' words, "I am the door" (John 10:9), and they wrought the sign of the Cross into every door they made. This is a very potent symbol, for the Cross is indeed the doorway into a fuller, more abundant life.

A new spirit of forgiveness

This is another aspect of the sacrifice which we are seeing in the present revival. Unforgiveness is often an obstacle to revival. It creeps up on us and causes powerlessness. Some say, "I will forgive them for what they did, but I cannot forget it." But true forgiveness also means forgetting. The words for forgiveness in both Hebrew and Greek literally mean "to put away" or "to send away for ever". I am deeply moved at the supreme sacrifice some are making, giving their lives away, obeying Jesus' command: "Forgive, and you will be forgiven."

Destroying idols

We are reminded again and again in Scripture that idols prevent us from receiving favour, blessing and revival from God. He said to Ezekiel, "Son of man, these men have set up idols in their hearts . . . Should I let them enquire of me at all?" (Ezekiel 14:3). God will resolutely turn his face from the prayers of all who cherish idols in their hearts. John said, "children, keep yourselves from idols" (1 John 5:21).

Many in our nation have deliberately turned away from the Lord, rejecting both Him and His Word. This wilful rejection of God and of His Son Jesus is the root of every evil which defiles our nation. In place of the true God people have chosen idols of their own making. The humanist and secularist thinkers have said we are our own gods, so people now worship their own ambitions and lusts. They have become materialists and worship money and possessions. They have glorified sex and have become obsessed with gratifying their sexual appetites. These false gods allow people to live as they like, without fear of God. But on the coming Judgement Day they will have to face Him.

The biggest idol in the UK is television! It keeps great numbers of believers from having a red-hot fervour for God. Soap operas like *Eastenders*, *Home and Away*, *Dallas*, *Neighbours* and *Coronation Street* grip a million Christians like a drug. When I was a boy Christians used to say things like, "See you at the prayer meeting, DV." Now the attitude of a lot of Christians is "See you at the prayer meeting if there's nothing on TV"!

Someone from St Timothy's Church in Fort Worth, Texas, wrote this very telling parody of the 23rd Psalm, called *The 23rd Channel*:

> The TV is my shepherd; I shall not want. It maketh me to lie down on the sofa: it leadeth me in the paths of sex and violence. Yea, though I walk in the shadow of Christian responsibilities, there will be no interruption: for the TV is with me; its cable and its remote control they comfort me. It prepareth a commercial before me in the presence of my worldliness: it anointeth my head with humanism and consumerism; my coveting runneth over. Surely laziness and superficiality shall follow me all the days of my life: and I will dwell in the house watching TV for ever.

The only sure way to avoid defilement by idols is to maintain at all times the freshness of our "first love" for the Saviour – to have, like Count Zinzendorf of Moravia, "one passion – Jesus, Jesus only". We need to embrace the attitude expressed in P. Gerhardt's beautiful verse:

Jesus, Thy boundless love to me
No thought can reach, no tongue declare.
Oh, knit my thankful heart to Thee,
And reign without a rival there.

A personal, passionate, all-absorbing love for and dedication to Christ is a mighty factor in bringing revival victory. If your heart's desire is revival, then "Delight yourself in the Lord and he will give you the desires of your heart" (Psalm 37:4). God has promised, "Because he hath set his love upon me . . . He shall call upon me, and I will answer him" (Psalm 91:14-15).

Britain has had no widespread revival for generations, mainly because Christians have worshipped idols such as money and respectability. *We must repent and turn away from our idols.* We must love the Lord with all our hearts. In my crusades we often hold bonfires at which people burn ungodly things such as occult paraphernalia and unedifying books and pop records, but it is much more important that there should be a *bonfire in the heart.* We need to let God burn up all the evil things which we cherish in our hearts. As Jesus said, "No-one can serve two masters" (Matthew 6:24). We cannot serve both God and the gods of this world.

An errand boy in London was once waiting in front of a house. He leaned over its iron gate, with his head and arms on one side and his body on the other. Suddenly someone who had not seen him there quickly opened the gate. The boy's neck was badly wrenched. He was Michael Faraday, who later became a great scientist and a much-loved man. Today many Christians are at last discovering what Faraday found – that it is a dangerous thing to be on two sides of a fence at the same time. They are casting away their idols and coming down totally on Christ's side.

Costly love

Another part of the sacrifice for revival is love – real, practical love. This is seen in many different guises. For example, Christians involved in the revival in the city of Gloucester take soup, clothes, blankets and the Gospel message to the homeless at night. Through their work 3,000 souls have been won on the streets. Their love-sacrifice involves hours of voluntary effort after a hard day's work, loss of sleep, cold, weariness, abuse, danger and long evenings away from home and family.

Love is one of the keys to the revival. It is a revival of love not only among Christians but also for the unsaved. Through that love we are reaching out to lost, hard, pagan people – black people and white people, rich and poor, religious and agnostic, intellectual and uneducated, Hindu, Moslem and Sikh, Protestant and Catholic. Our hearts are overflowing with Christ's love – and His love "never fails" (1 Corinthians 13:8).

The sacrifice of time

I often hear Christians say things like, "We're too busy – we haven't got the time. We can't get involved." Few Christians make time for Christ's work, and that is one of the reasons why we have had no revival for the past forty years! But things are changing – today many Christians are working day and night for Jesus, living every hour for Him.

Whether our responsibilities are great or small, as followers of Christ we must obey His command to seek first His Kingdom and His righteousnss (Matthew 6:33). A Christian might argue that he is swamped by the demands of his business, the cost of living, the needs of his growing family, and so on. But the Saviour understands all that and will provide all our needs. What He asks is that we put His Kingdom first in our lives, that we give our time up to Him.

I believe that to some extent the Restoration Movement has encouraged laziness. The emphasis has been on getting your own house in order – putting your family and church first. So for the last fifteen years the ideal of hard work for the Lord in evangelism has been neglected. The Movement has been rather inward looking. Of course, building your family and church is very important, but haven't things gone too far? In the new revival these concerns are balanced by a renewed emphasis on being saved to serve. People are giving their time to God sacrificially, and so their work is having a great impact.

Patience

Patience is today a lost art, and yet it is so important in God's work. Susannah Wesley, one of the seventeenth century's outstanding evangelical leaders, was once asked how she had the patience to teach a child the same thing over and over again twenty times. She replied, "If I stayed at only nineteen times and gave up, I should have lost my labour, for it was the twentieth time that fixed it." Often only patience and perseverance in a task will produce results. Nine years of patient work had to be done before the first New Zealand Maori was converted. It took Dr Johnson seven years to get his first Burmese convert. In Tahiti sixteen years passed before any of the people were saved. Thus we can see great patience in the work of some of the pioneer missionaries of the past.

James wrote, "Perseverance [or patience] must finish its work so that you may be mature and complete, not lacking anything" (James 1:4). David waited seven and a half years for his throne, but in God's time he had it.

Patience is often the answer to our problems. If we simply wait, the enemy's fury is spent and we conserve our strength to win the battle in the end.

We need to have patience in prayer. I have so often found that this pays off. Since I started preaching the Gospel at the age of seventeen I have often wondered, "When will the revival come? Why hasn't it come already?" But God has taught me to be patient. This is the Scripture He has often given me over the years: "Let us not become weary of doing good, for at the proper time we will reap a harvest if we do not give up" (Galatians 6:9). Now is the proper time – the reaping has begun!

Over the decades these scriptures have sustained me: "Wait on the Lord and keep his way. He will exalt you to possess the land" (Psalm 37:34); "the revelation awaits an appointed time . . . Though it linger, wait for it; it will certainly come and not delay" (Habakkuk 2:3); "You need to persevere [have patience] so that when you have done the will of God, you will receive what he has promised" (Hebrews 10:36); "God . . . acts on behalf of those who wait for him" (Isaiah 64:4).

My wife Lilian and I have toiled all over the world, winning souls, healing the sick in Jesus' name, casting out devils, building churches, planting new fellowships. We prayed, watched and waited for revival in the UK. We often wondered, "When is it going to happen, God? Why are you tarrying?" We had the Billy Graham crusades: they were greatly blessed by God, but they did not bring revival. Then other evangelists came – but still no revival. Then came the charismatic renewal, and our hopes lifted enormously – only to be dashed later, when it became clear that the renewal was for most part going to influence only the Church and would have little impact upon the nation as a whole. Then we had the house church movement, but again it was mainly Christians who were blessed by it. It is only now that we are beginning to see signs of true revival in this country. God is faithful: we waited patiently, and now we are seeing what we have been praying for all these years. I thank God for the long patience of the saints who have throughout this time waited, and whose persistent prayers have helped to bring the fire down to this country today. We are experiencing this outpouring because of the patience of a few saints over many years.

Recently I have been working in the Cotswolds area and seeing a large response from the wealthy, landowning, horse-racing set and also from people of more modest means – including many Gypsies. Scores of them have been converted in this area, and we are seeing a wonderful Gospel breakthrough among these people. I preached in this very same area when I started my ministry at the age of seventeen, working with a veteran Wiltshire preacher known as "Old Cox", but it has taken over thirty years for me to reap a harvest. I sowed patiently, I toiled, I prayed, I waited, and finally God has granted signs and wonders, opening the eyes of the people of the Cotswolds.

Let us not think, as we plead for revival, that we have to move God to share our concern and burden about the matter. We feel as we do because God has stirred us to share a fraction of His concern. Our longing is but a pale, feeble reflction of His own. Our exercise of patience should draw us into a deeper relationship with "the God of patience", who has manifested such longsuffering towards the sons of men. How long did He wait for us before we began to wait for Him? Let us also remember that for nigh on 2,000 years the Son has been at the Father's right hand engaged in this very ministry of praying and waiting, and He will continue in it until His enemies are made his footstool (Hebrews 10:13).

Just as the first outpouring of the Spirit at Pentecost was the basic blueprint for every subsequent outpouring, so the preparation for Pentecost constitutes a pattern for our preparation today. The apostles were charged by Christ to "wait for the gift my Father promised, which you heard me speak about" (Acts 1:4). So they waited, continuing steadfastly in prayer until the Day of Pentcost came. We too must wait and pray.

The mark of a vital faith is that it endures. God wants us to have what He has promised, but we can only have it by a faith which has been purified and perfected through the exercise of patience. Abraham, "after waiting patiently . . . received what was promised" (Hebrews 6:15). But he was not unique; there have been many saints who have obtained blessing from God in the same way.

So let us "imitate those who through faith and patience inherit what has been promised" (6:12).

Thankfulness

Part of the cost of revival is having a heart which is full of thanks to God. Thanksgiving is one of the hallmarks of the present move of God. It is wonderful to see the thankful, joyful, sweet Christians whom God is raising up in the revival fellowships. They are people for whom praise is a whole lifestyle. The powers of darkness are neutralized, banned, shaken and put to flight by a praising, thankful, prayerful heart. The devil is allergic to thanksgiving.

In this present revival we are teaching our converts that when they are faced with discouragement, sickness, stress, misunderstanding and persecution they should look to Jesus and thank Him with all their hearts. He said, "Blessed are you when people insult you, persecute you and say all kinds of evil against you because of me. Rejoice and be glad, for great is your reward in heaven" (Matthew 5:11-12).

In one town the worshippers from an unrenewed church went to a coffee shop for refreshments after their Sunday service, but found that the Christians from the local revival church were there, singing to God and thanking Him aloud for His goodness. It could be heard out in the street! The people from the traditional church went to their vicar to complain about this, since they felt that it was inappropriate to praise God in a common public place.

Many biblical characters challenge us by their thankful

attitude. David, the psalmist, never tires of thanking God. His testimony is heart-warming: "The Lord is my strength and my shield; my heart trusts in him, and I am helped. My heart leaps for joy and I will give thanks to him in song" (Psalm 28:7). Nor did David limit his thanksgiving to his private devotions: "I will give you thanks in the great assembly; among throngs of people I will praise you" (35:18). Being thankful to God himself, he used all his powers of persuasion to excite others to thank the Lord. Over the centuries the Holy Spirit has used David's writings to teach people to thank God worthily.

Paul was a thankful man. His gratitude to the Lord shone through his life of sacrificial service and obedience. "Be joyful always," he wrote; "pray continually; give thanks in all circumstances, for this is God's will for you in Christ Jesus" (1 Thessalonians 5:16-18); "Devote yourselves to prayer, being watchful and thankful" (Colossians 4:2). This man of revival, this man who could pray in an amazing way, this man who could get extraordinary miracles and staggering results, was a thankful, praising, rejoicing person. Far from diminishing with the passage of time, his thankfulness blossomed as the years went by. Paul was so busy thanking God that he had no time to wallow in his trying experiences.

If we have a praising and thankful spirit, our faith is quickened in a remarkable way, and thus the spiritual power which carries out what we are praying for is released. This was so in the case of Abraham, who "was strengthened in his faith and gave glory to God" (Romans 4:20). Scripture records that three times a day Daniel "got down on his knes and prayed, giving thanks to his God" (Daniel 6:10). It was this prayer and thankfulness which shut the mouths of the lions in the den. Praise strengthens prayer and produces an attitude of victorious intercession. At Philippi Paul and Silas were imprisoned, but the midnight hour found them "praying and singing hymns to God" (Acts 16:25), with the other prisoners as their silent, wondering audience. Then a mighty earthquake shook the foundations of the prison, opened all the doors and loosed everyone's chains. As a result the jailer and his entire household were immediately converted. I am sure that the spiritual "earthquakes" we are witnessing in the revival are partly due to the great spirit of thanks and praise which is among the Christians involved.

Be a thankful Christian! Thank God for delivering you from guilt, for giving you peace of mind, for the way He leads you and guides you in life. Above all, thank Him for who He is and for His glorious character. Also thank Him for the future – thank Him for His plans for you and for what you can become through Him. Jam your prayers with thankful statements! I have always found that fatigue, despair, defeat, difficulties and spiritual blockages have all evaporated through a praising attitude. Andrew Murray, the saintly Keswick preacher, said, "To be thankful for what I have from the Lord . . . is the surest way to receive more." Remember that in heaven we will be singing endless praises to God: "Praise and glory and wisdom and thanks and honour and power and strength be to our God for ever and ever. Amen!" (Revelation 7:12).

Daring and risk

Daring and risk are part of the cost of the revival. To see results we must be daring – we must be prepared to take a risk. The motto of the SAS is "Who Dares Wins", and that could easily apply to God's people. President Roosevelt said, "Better to dare some mighty things and go checkered by some failures . . . than not dare . . . and rank with those who enjoy neither victory nor defeat."

Recently I preached at a large rally at Arnhem in Holland, the scene of one of the most bloody and desperate battles of the Second World War. Here in 1944 thousands of British paratroopers landed in a bid to take the Arnhem bridges and so shorten the war by six months. The mission failed, and only a few of our soldiers got back safely. But, as one of the memorials at Arnhem says, "Through their daring, their names will live forever."

We must be daring in our attacks upon the enemy, but we must also be daring in our prayer. God wants us to be bold, trusting that He will answer our prayers. As the writer of Hebrews said, "Let us then approach the throne of grace with confidence, so that we may receive mercy and find grace to help us in our time of need" (4:16). How often we keep the Almighty standing by in silent inactivity, with all the power of the universe in His hands. He yearns to intervene, to demonstrate His power and reveal His glory, but He cannot while we fail to ask as we should, while we are earthbound in our thinking, working and praying! No wonder the Lord says, "If my people would but listen to me, if Israel would follow my ways, how quickly would I subdue their enemies and turn my hand against their foes!" (Psalm 81:13-14). God wants us to have a bold faith. Such a faith does not stagger at His promises – rather, it opens the windows of heaven for revival. Such a faith delights God's heart.

In this revival we are asking big, daring things of God. As John Newton wrote:

Thou art coming to a King –
Large petitions with thee bring;
For His grace and power are such,
None can ever ask too much.

Many great risks are being taken in this present move of God. Remember – there is no faith where there is no risk.

Intercession

To see revival come we need to have the spiritual stamina to persevere in intercession. We need to pray the way Paul meant when he wrote: "pray in the Spirit on all occasions with all kinds of prayers and requests. With this in mind, be alert and always keep on praying for all the saints" (Ephesians 6:18). But this stamina is rare, and the temptation to give up is great. Jesus' disciples were tempted in this way. Luke tells us that He "told his disciples a parable to show them that they should always pray and not give up" (Luke 18:1). Over the past sixty years many intercessors have given up, and so revival has been delayed.

We need to remember that "our struggle is not against flesh and blood, but against the rulers, against the authorities, against the powers of this dark world and against the spiritual forces of evil in the heavenly realms" (Ephesians 6:12). The prayer warrior faces an enemy with immense spiritual resources and centuries of experience in spiritual conflict. He is engaged in a battle to the death. When the devil cannot win by a frontal assault, he will use a flank attack or fifth-column tactics. When he cannot intimidate us as a roaring lion, he will come as an angel of light to beguile us. What a need there is for vigilance!

Multitudes are desperate, lying in utter darkness, waiting for the light. Only our prayers will bring the light to them. In the days of Ezekiel the Lord said, "I looked for a man among them who would . . . stand before me in the gap on behalf of the land" (Ezekiel 22:30), and He is looking for such people today. God is looking for intercessors who will live a life of crucifixion, laying down their lives daily for the cause of Christ. You and I must stand in the gap for the unsaved. The Lord is now calling for more intercessors! Offer yourself – join the army of prayer warriors!

I used to know a lady living in the West Country who was one of those self-sacrificing intercessors. Her health was failing, but she had a clear vision of the need for revival and a great prayer burden for it. Her sister believes that she actually hastened her own death through her tireless and agonized prayer that the windows of heaven might be opened. It is people like that who are turning the tide for God.

The financial cost

There is a close link between financial giving and revival. Many of the Christians who are involved in the present revival are making big financial sacrifices for it. I know of people who have sold their homes and moved into smaller houses, giving the profit they have made to God's work. I know of people who have given their life's savings so that souls might be won and new churches might be opened. Such folk never go without, but are blessed by God in a way that mean, critical, money-grabbing people cannot understand.

God requires us to be willing to sacrifice our money. If we put His work first, He will take care of our financial needs. Jesus said, "Seek first his kingdom and his righteousness, and all these things [i.e. the money we need] will be given to you as well" (Matthew 6:33).

A. W. Tozer wrote:

> Money often comes between men and God. Someone has said that you can take two small ten-cent pieces, just two dimes, and shut out the view of a panoramic landscape. Go to the mountains and just hold two coins closely in front of your eyes – the mountains are still there, but you cannot see them at all because there is a dime shutting off the vision in each eye.

You can easily tell how much a person loves the Saviour by how readily he surrenders his money to Him. Anyone who complains and criticizes when asked to give to God's work cannot be in a right spiritual state. If they are not right with God, then they will not be instrumental in bringing about revival.

We need to get this matter into its proper perspective. God is so generous to us! He not only blesses us with salvation, health, happy families and a stress-free life, but He also allows us to keep 90% of our earnings for ourselves. What a kind God He is, and how mean it is of us to deny Him what He wants from us!

Consecration

I have been in the ministry for thirty-six years. In that time I have worked hard, slogging from town to town, often with little help. My wife and I have been no strangers to hardship, tiredness, rejection, unkindness, apathy, indifference and misunderstanding. At times we have been depressed, and sometimes we have found the cares and duties of family life very tiring. The trials, testings, failures and mistakes have been numerous and often shattering. But through all of this we have learned by God's grace to walk in His presence and to carry that presence with us. Over a period of time I was deeply chastened by God, and as a result I began to discover new dimensions of spirituality and a fresh sense of God's reality. He had allowed me to come to a stage where I was utterly at His disposal, inflamed and ready to do battle for Him. Out of the ashes of heartfelt repentance I had arisen with a new readiness. By 1990 I was completely consecrated to God and to His work. As God melted me and I found others of like mind, the flame of revival was lit and began to burn.

God will bring revival through those who are consecrated to Him. When even a minority of believers are consecrated to God, it is possible to have a revival, and this is what is happening in the UK today.

Sadly, some Christians, faced with the utter consecration of those caught up in the revival, have fallen away. One man, who had been advised to turn his life over to Jesus, became very angry. He had no desire to confess his sins and put his life in order. Finally he said at a meeting, "I'm going home. All this praying is getting me down. I refuse to have anything to do with this fanatical type of Christianity!" Compromising, double-minded Christians like that fall out of the race.

Consecration was vital to the revivals of the past. A man was once researching the life of George Fox, the founder of the Society of Friends. When asked to sum up Fox's character, he replied, "The secret of George Fox's life is easily told: he was completely master of himself because he was completely a servant of God."

God must have first place in our lives. Our love for Him must be our first love. Arthur Wallis wrote:

> Of all the offerings we may bring to the Lord, the expression of our heart's affection is supreme. He cannot accept any substitute for this . . . He is not content to accept the second best. He will brook no rival for that first place in the heart. "He that loveth father or mother (or anyone else) more than Me is not worthy of Me" (Matthew 10:37).

Paul wrote, "I urge you, brothers, in view of God's mercy, to offer your bodies as living sacrifces, holy and pleasing to God – which is your spiritual worship" (Romans 12:1). This is what Watchman Nee meant by the term, "the normal Christian life" – by this definition most Christians' lives are sub-normal!

To be fully consecrated to God means to place yourself fully into His hands; it means that you no longer belong to yourself; it means that God is your one and only Master. God decides your plans and aims in life, and your will becomes totally His. All that remains for you to do is to obey Him. As the godly Chinese Christian leader Wong Ming Dao said, consecration "means the road you follow is the one He commands you to follow, the work you undertake is the work that He directs you in, your location is where the Lord places you".

But we do not necessarily need to be in full-time

Christian work in order to be fully consecrated. Every believer should be working "full time" for the Lord in the sense of living totally for Him, but most Christians are called to remain in secular employment.

C. T. Studd, the great pioneer missionary of the last century, gave up his family fortune in order to be able to seek God totally. He sought revival and sacrificed his life on the altar. He gave himself away for Christ and poured out his life in God's service. He wrote these challenging words:

> Don't seek a long life – Christ had a short one. Don't live in luxury – Christ lived and died poor. Don't live for pleasure – Christ pleased not himself. Don't live for fame – Christ made himself of no reputation. Don't live at ease – Christ suffered for you the shame, the scourge and the cross. Don't lose your opportunity and inherit an eternity of shame and regrets hereafter.

Studd was willing to pay the price, and as a result there was a great revival in Africa. Only a few in Britain today are paying such a price. But God is using those few for His glory. I urge you to join this heroic band of saints!

We will not be liked for our full consecration, but God is calling us to it. He is looking for people who are utterly given over to Him, who are willing to fight for Him. Through them He will manifest His truth and might. The time is right for such people to speak out in this nation with God's power and authority.

CHAPTER 16

Obstacles to Revival

Whosoever he be of you that renounceth not all that he hath, he cannot be my disciple.

(Luke 14:33)

In many places in the world I have seen powerful revivals taking place – sovereign, divine visitations flowing straight from the throne of God. Why is it that we have not seen revival like that in Britain? Because of the shortcomings of the Church in this country. In this chapter we will take a look at some of them.

Are we prepared to work?

Christian people here are so easily satisfied! As soon as a church congregation see a few people saved, they think they can relax for the next couple of years. People speak in tongues a little and there are a few healings, and they think they have everything. Some years ago the leaders of a church in England wrote to me saying that they did not need any more evangelistic or healing missions. They now had a hundred people in their congregation and could handle no more – and this in a town with a population of 75,000! More than one church has asked me to postpone a planned visit for a year or two because the previous visit has left them with so many converts that they cannot manage any more new people for a while. How pathetic! What a sad lack of passion and vision!

In order for revival to come, God's people must be prepared to work. At some churches where I preach the Christians seem to hope that my visit will by itself induce enthusiasm. They think I can produce revival out of my suitcase, just like Aladdin releasing his genie by rubbing his lamp. They do nothing to prepare themselves. They are lethargic, lazy and icy cold in spirit. They expect a visiting preacher to wave his magic wand, work ten miracles and fill their church with converts. This is the case even in some charismatic churches. They sing catchy songs, dance in the aisles, wave their hands and read from the Bible, but really their "renewal" has become a kind "orthodoxy" – a formula which is not working. They have little hunger for God and are not committed to intercession. They hardly know what I'm talking about when I speak of the agonized, earnest, intense, passionate prayer which is the essential precursor of revival.

God is raising up a people who have persistence and zeal – people who are born again and sanctified and who long for revival and are prepared to pay the necessary price for it. Revival does not come to the diluted, feeble form of Christianity which is found in so many churches; it comes as a result of nights spent in prayer and fasting. God will move to bless the sincere, soul-seeking, prayerful heart.

The great C. H. Spurgeon prayed:

> O Thou art God, answer us by fire, we pray Thee! Answer us both by *wind and fire*, and then we shall see Thee to be God indeed. The kingdom comes not,

and the work is flagging. Oh, that Thou wouldst send *the wind and the fire!* . . . Oh, for a sweep of the wind that will set the sea in motion . . . Oh, for the fire to fall again – fire which shall affect the most stolid! Oh, that such fire might first sit upon the disciples, and then fall on all around! O God, Thou art ready to work with us today even as Thou didst then. Stay not, we beseech Thee, but work at once. Break down every barrier that hinders the incoming of Thy might! Give us now both hearts of flame and tongues of fire . . . Amen!

Accepting the light

One dark night in Edinburgh the six-year-old Robert Louis Stevenson looked out of his bedroom window at the street below. He excitedly called to his nurse, "Look, look!" She came to the window. Down below the lamp lighter was working his way along the street with his long pole, setting each streetlamp aflame. The boy said, "Look at that man going down the street making holes in the dark!" That is exactly what revival does; it makes holes in the darkness of this world. It brings light into the darkened areas of our society. But sadly, many Christians have become so accustomed to the dark that they cannot accept the light when it comes. They cannot recognize God's new blessings and movings.

Will the Christians in the Church in Britain recognize and accept the revival which has now come? Some of them cannot or will not, since it does not fit in with their thinking or their particular denominational programmes. Perhaps they expect it to be "charismatic" in a narrow sense; perhaps they think it will be one big Bible meeting or worship session. Perhaps they are expecting it to be like Luther's sixteenth-century Restoration, or Wesley's eighteenth-century revival, or one of the moves of God in Victorian times. Some Christians are rejecting the revival because it means change, upheaval and loss of pride for them, and they do not want any of that.

Many Christians are looking for revival, but they are looking for it in the wrong place: they expect it to happen according to their preconceived notions. Don't let yourself be bypassed by God's blessing when it comes, just because it has not come the way you expected it to. Enoch saw revival in his time, and was then swept up to heaven by God. Noah, the next revivalist, waited patiently, expecting God to do the same thing for him, but no – instead God told him to build an ark. God is a God of variety.

William Reid wrote,

> We may not all dream the same dream. We may not all express in the same way the newborn hope that has arisen in our hearts . . . It may be when the veil is drawn asunder, when the time has come for God to act and to take the cataract off the eyes of the nation, that the mode and the method of the great ministry of the Spirit of God, for a great out-pouring, shall be very *different* from what we see and feel and hear today.

The history of revivals shows very clearly that God often acts in an unexpected way, working not necessarily through ministers but perhaps through people who may regard themselves as very insignificant members of the Church.

God will probably not work in quite the way we

imagined, but one thing is sure: the revival He sends will exceed all our expectations. Paul affirmed that God was "able to do immeasurably more than all we ask or imagine, according to his power that is at work within us" (Ephesians 3:20).

Recently many people have asked me whether I think this revival will be limited in scope or widespread. Will the fire burn brightly in isolated areas or will it spread all over the country? Will it last a long time or will it fade out? I think the area and duration of the revival depend entirely upon our prayer life – upon our continued dedication, obedience, discipline and openness to what God wants of us. *God is willing to send revival*, but we must be prepared to pray.

I believe that the revival will be widespread, but, while it will find many open, accepting hearts, it will also be rejected by others. Some Christians will completely miss what God is doing in this nation now. They will grieve the Holy Spirit by their negativism, doubt, criticism, fault-finding gossip, coldness of heart, apathy, jealousy and formalism. They will block the move of God by not hungering for Him and seeking after Him, by not coming to Him now, while He is drawing, warning, convincing and saving people in great numbers and in many places. Many will miss the revival through sheer churchy, denominational pride, by living in the past and failing to keep pace with the Holy Spirit.

A Church handicapped by sin

Where there is no Christian voice, no prophetic word, the Gospel diminishes and the darkness gets darker. A silent Church which does not reach the people in deep darkness and cares only for its own folk is failing to fulfil God's plans both for itself and for the world. The Church should have penetrated the darkness, but instead the darkness has infiltrated the Church. Materialism, love of money, greediness, worldliness, prayerlessness, jealousy, politicking, pride, sexual permissiveness and addictions defile the lives of many believers. And the sin is not confined to the sheep of the flock but is to be found in the hearts of the shepherds too. Amongst ministers the biggest sin is selling out the anointing of God for prestige and position. These sins are the things which have brought us to defeat. The Church is at the mercy of the enemy and the world.

Sin in the camp is destroying the effectiveness of God's people. Psalm 66 says, "If I had cherished sin in my heart, the Lord would not have listened" (verse 18). But the toleration and cherishing of sin is exactly what has happened in the Church. Unjudged and unforgiven sin makes fellowship with God impossible. This is obvious the moment we consider His character. "God is light; in him there is no darkness at all. If we claim to have fellowship with him yet walk in the darkness, we lie and do not live by the truth" (1 John 1:5). It was to the Lord's own people that Isaiah had to say, "your iniquities have separated you from your God; your sins have hidden his face from you, so that he will not hear" (Isaiah 59:2).

Why has the modern Church seen so much defeat? Why has the condition of so many believers been so pitiful? Why have so many who have served the Lord lost power? Because of sin. Had it not been for the sin in the Church, the Lord would have sent revival to Britain long ago. The fulfilment of God's promises will be seriously hindered and our work for Him will not have any outstanding results until the Church's hidden sins are dealt with.

Sadly, it is true that there are many churches where human sin will block the coming of revival, or where that sin will kill revival soon after its birth. A while ago I led a mission in a certain church. Despite the lackadaisical attitude of most of the congregation God moved and many people were converted. But after the mission was over some people started to complain about what had happened. When I investigated later I discovered that one of the principal bones of contention was the fact that the church's carpet had been spoiled during the mission by the copious tears of those who had been convicted of sin by God! How awful, heartless, hard and terrible! Is it any wonder that the revival in that church soon died out? There is no revival for such people.

This nation is desperate. They look to the Church, but they find no help there. The Baptists are too busy baptizing; the Methodists are too busy with their social charters; the Anglicans are too busy debating what to do about women's ministry and how to deal with their heretical bishops; the house churches are tied up in their shepherding; the Free Churches are bogged down in their Calvinism; the Reformed Churches are too busy worrying about liberalism; the Assemblies of God are hindered by a spirit of caution regarding signs, wonders and miracles . . . In every denomination there are major obstacles to true revival, and at the root of all those obstacles is self-doubt.

One of the most widespread sins in the Church is complacency – accepting things the way they are. A young preacher was about to become the minister of a certain fellowship, and just before his induction service he spent some time walking the streets surrounding the church. He noted the crowded pubs, the nightclubs, the gambling places, the blue cinemas, the pornographic magazines on display in the newsagents' shops; he even heard little children swearing in the streets. Arriving at the church shortly before the service was due to start, he went into the vestry and wept! A few minutes later one of the deacons came in and noticed that the young preacher's eyes were red. The deacon asked him what the matter was. "Oh, it's all those lost people out there," he replied. "Don't worry about it," said the deacon. "You'll get used to it." Are we like that deacon? Have we got used to the sin which is all around us and in our own lives? Have we concluded that nothing can be done about it? Have we accepted the ugly status quo?

Compromize and sin are so ingrained in the life of the Church that it is often difficult to preach the Word of God truly and faithfully. Many want a softly-softly, easy-going Christianity. A pastor in Adelaide in Australia once asked me to preach something "less stinging" and "more gentle". But a true Gospel preacher cannot cease from preaching the whole doctrine of God. As a result he will often suffer invective, castigation, misunderstanding and cries of "Exaggeration!" But God's call and commission drive us on, and His grace enables us to go on preaching the full Gospel.

Yes, we all want to be liked and respected, to be approved of and welcomed everywhere. But if a preacher is preaching the clear, apostolic Word of God, if he is talking straight, then he won't be popular with everyone. One minister once told me that I make one enemy and two friends every time I preach!

The need for repentance

Many people want revival – they want to see astounding miracles and signs – but they don't want to do the necessary groundwork first. We only see the great sweep of the Holy Spirit where there has first been humble confession of sin and passionate praying. We must search our hearts, and let God search them, so that anything which hinders revival may be removed. In the past I have sometimes cancelled preaching appointments, interviews and social gatherings in order to be able to spend a week in my caravan in the countryside seeking God. Those times have always been invigourating and life-changing! We need to pray with the psalmist: "search me, O God, and know my heart; test me and know my anxious thoughts. See if there is any offensive way in me, and lead me in the way everlasting" (Psalm 139:23-24).

The Bible says, "He who conceals his sins does not prosper, but whoever confesses and renounces them finds mercy" (Proverbs 28:13). If we attempt to cover our sins up, our hearts become hard. Sadly, this is what has happened to many Christian leaders. They have become hardened through compromize and cover-up. Their followers have thus become accustomed to an impure spirit in their churches – to an unnatural, non-revival atmosphere. It is better to be disparaged before men for our sins than to cover up. Temporary dishonour is better than abiding in hidden sin. If we are blatantly honest we will be ten feet taller and more trusted and respected by others. If we confess our sins God will be able to bring revival through us!

CHAPTER 17
An Opposed Revival

When men speak ill of thee, live so that nobody will believe them.

(Plato)

Opposition is inevitable

You know a revival is a true revival if it is meeting opposition. The Gospel is an offence to sinful humanity, and when it is preached uncompromizingly it provokes a sharp reaction.

There is a stigma attached to the Gospel. If we are faithful to it we will experience opposition, disgrace and shame. That was what the apostles found: they "left the Sanhedrin, rejoicing because they had been counted worthy of suffering disgrace for the name" (Acts 5:41). Some people have tried to preach a destigmatized and popularized gospel. But that is impossible: such a gospel is not the true Gospel, which will always be an offence to the world and to a carnal, unbelieving, worldly Church. As Jesus said, "Woe to you when all men speak well of you, for that is how their fathers treated the false prophets" (Luke 6:26).

The Gospel message is not always ular. People are

offended when they hear that they are sinful. Do you remember the uproar there was a few years ago when John Anderton, the Chief Constable of Greater Manchester, said that AIDS was a disease normally "brought on by sinful living"? And yet he was quite right to say that. There will be opposition when we declare God's pure Word in an impure world.

Many good Christian leaders have suffered great persecution in Europe in recent years – and not just in the communist countries. In Norway the Pentecostal preacher Nistrom was imprisoned for calling homosexuality a sin. To describe it in such terms is against the law of that land! In Denmark Dr Harriett has been struck off the register for making a stand against abortion. In Sweden the preacher Ulk Ulkman was fined for telling his congregation that if necessary they should discipline their children by smacking. Are you and I willing to go to jail for Christ, if it should ever come to that?

I was recently working in a crusade in a West Country city. There was scarcely any support from the local churches. They had all said they were too busy to be involved. However, a Moslem allowed us to hold our meetings in his nightclub free of charge! There were 130 conversions and many healings. The county paper carried a story about the crusade on its centre pages. However, the local churches missed the whole thing. One canon attacked what he called "itinerant preachers". I said during the crusade that Islam was a false religion, and this got me on TV. However, the Mayor opposed me, calling for racial harmony. Hundreds of letters poured in, three quarters of them agreeing with what I had said. Most of the evangelical pastors in the area remained silent during the attacks and hullabaloo, but a Brethren elder and a Baptist minister supported me. I appeared on TV again and repeated my earlier assertion. "Christ is the *only* Saviour," I said. "Anyone who preaches that there is another way to the Father is preaching a false gospel." In another town in the West Country the local churches ganged up and offered us hundreds of pounds if we would promise not to come and preach!

If you are involved in the revival, all sorts of untruths will be said about you. I have been criticized because I have mixed with Roman Catholics and Hindus and Moslems. I have been accused of being anti-church and of being too ecumenical!

A couple of years ago I was talking with Tom Woods, a prophet who has been greatly used by God. He died recently in his nineties. As we were talking he suddenly laid his hands on me roughly and said, "You are going into the darkness! But don't fear – great light is around you, and as you move forward with God the light increases. No foe can touch you – the light drives back the darkness!"

Why are some Christians so stunned when they are mistreated and slandered? Do they expect better treatment from the world than our Master received? Jesus was condemned by many of His contemporaries, and finally they killed Him. He told us, "If the head of the house has been called Beelzebub, how much more the members of his household!" (Matthew 10:25).

True revival means a head-on collision with the devil. Some believers don't like that – they don't want to suffer for Jesus, for truth, for Scripture, for spiritual things, for the blood of Christ, for the baptism in the Holy Ghost, for the will of God, for revival. They are offended and embarassed by the enthusiasm, dedication and total sacrifice of those who are involved in the revival.

Opposition from Christians

Some of those who oppose the revival are Christians. They are those who "strain out a gnat but swallow a camel" (Matthew 23:24); they tithe a tenth of their mint but "neglect justice and the love of God" (Luke 11:42). They profess much and possess little; they have all the right expressions but few of the right experiences. We read in Micah 7:6, "a man's enemies are the members of his own household". These words of James Robe apply to some Christians today: "Can you find it in your hearts to be like the Jews, who prayed and longed for the coming of the Messiah, and when He came, rejected and crucified Him, because He came not in the way their prejudices led them to look for Him?"

Some Christians cannot accept what God is doing in the revival. They come to the meetings to find things to criticize and gossip about, and they go away untouched and unmoved. Even some ministers are like that. They say, "It's all an exaggeration – there's nothing in it!" They cannot see the hand of God at work, and so they miss the revival. They have become so accustomed to not having mighty visitations of God in their churches that they can no longer recognize them when they do come elsewhere. They believe that if such things do not happen in their churches, then they do not happen at all. Pride reigns in the hearts of thousands of born-again believers, many of them ministers. They think they have a monopoly on God. What a foolish attitude! If I hear of an outbreak of blessing anywhere I jump into my car and get to where it's happening as fast as I can!

In this present revival we are seeing mighty, miraculous manifestations of God's power. However, some Christians find this hard to accept. They may pray for revival for years, and yet when it comes they reject it. Why? Because it is accompanied by healings, speaking in tongues and other supernatural happenings. This is a tragic mistake: we should accept and rejoice in whatever God does, even if it is not quite what we have been expecting. Duncan Campbell, speaking of the Hebridean revival, had these words of wisdom to offer: "Physical manifestations and prostrations have been a further feature. I find it somewhat difficult to explain this aspect, indeed I cannot; but this I will say, that the person who would associate this with satanic influence is coming perilously near to committing the unpardonable sin." Lady Huntingdon once wrote to George Whitefield on the subject of people falling down and crying out in his meetings. She advised him not to remove them from the meetings, as he had been doing. She said this put a damper on the Holy Spirit's activity. "You are making a great mistake," she wrote. "Don't be wiser than God. Let them cry out; it will do a great deal more good than your preaching."

We preachers shouldn't be too insistent that our meetings should go precisely according to plan; sometimes God will want to do something different. At one revival meeting a man in the audience suddenly stood up when I was preaching. I was near the end of my message on the atonement of Christ and was about to ask the people to think seriously about what I had said and to surrender themselves to Christ. But before I could do this the man started shouting, "What have I got to do to get this blessing you've been talking about?" He was well dressed and he was not rude or rowdy; he had a cultured Oxford accent, in fact. But he was very agitated. "Where can I find this blessing?" he called out. I told him he had to repent and believe. He pushed his way forward eagerly to give his life to Christ. He was swiftly followed by two thirds of the congregation! God had wanted to move a little faster than I had intended!

This sort of thing is happening more and more in revival meetings. This is nothing new, of course. True revivals have always been marked by powerful and widespread outpourings of the Holy Spirit. On many occasions preachers have had to end their sermons abruptly because their hearers have fallen down under the power of the Spirit or because their sermons have been drowned out by cries for mercy. In the present revival prostrations and the like have been very beneficial: they have caught the attention of both the Church and the world, and they have also greatly blessed the people who have been prostrated. However, some Christians regard this sort of thing as hysteria and mere human excitement. They make the mistake of judging revival by the standards of cold, correct formalism.

The sad thing about opposition is the harm it does to the opposers. Most of those who have opposed my ministry (many of them ministers) are now in a sorry state. Some have resigned from the ministry, others have been defrocked, and others are either dead or in mental homes. One has even been struck dumb!

How to respond to opposition

It is important that we should not have a persecution mania. Not all criticism is malicious; some of it may be constructive. We need to know the difference. Constructive criticism should always be considered carefully; rebuke and reproof may be profitable.

One of the greatest temptations for those involved in the revival is to be sidetracked into time-wasting defence of one's reputation. This is one of the enemy's wearing-down tactics. How must we respond to it? We must simply get on with the task of rescuing precious souls from the everlasting clutches of the devil. Watchman Nee said:

> Let all brothers and sisters learn this lesson: the man of authority whom God establishes is able to endure provocation. If the authority you possess cannot be offended, you are qualified to be in authority . . . Let no one defend himself nor speak for himself. Learn to wait and to be humble before God . . . The lower one prostrates himself before God, the quicker the Lord will vindicate him.

Let us be clear about one thing: slander and malice and opposition will not put a stop to the revival. Oh no! With faith, love and perseverance we must simply "sit it out". Charles Finney observed:

> While we keep humble, and in prayerful spirit, while we do not retaliate, but possess our souls in patience, while we do not suffer ourselves to be diverted, to recriminate, and grieve away the spirit of prayer, the work will go forward. But the minute a preacher

begins to think that the opposition is no longer to be tolerated and he must reply, he has become diverted.

We should not be discouraged by opposition. Jesus will not forsake us. If we rest in Him we cannot fail. He said, "In this world you will have trouble. But take heart! I have overcome the world" (John 16:33).

Charles H. Spurgeon said, "As sure as ever God puts His children in the furnace, He will be in the furnace with them." God is always with His people, protecting them. He is never caught off guard. He is always in front of His people and never gets left behind.

I teach the people in the revival not to be frightened by the devil's tricks. He is a con-man – he tries to divide, divert, disappoint and discourage believers. Fear is his standard weapon, a poison brewed in hell. He wants the lives of Christians to be full of fear every day. But in the Name of Jesus we can overcome fear. He said, "I have given you authority to trample on snakes and scorpions, and to overcome all the power of the enemy; nothing will harm you" (Luke 10:19).

The believer will inevitably experience trials. The Scripture says, "Blessed is the man who perseveres under trial, because when he has stood the test, he will receive the crown of life that God has promised to those who love him" (James 1:12). God allows trials to come to us so that we will learn to be people of faith. Someone once said, "A Christian is like a teabag – he's not much good until he's been in some hot water."

James said, "Consider it pure joy, my brothers, whenever you face trials of many kinds, because you know that the testing of your faith develops perseverance"

(James 1:2). J. B. Phillips paraphrased these words as follows: "When all kinds of trials and temptations crowd into your lives . . . don't resent them as intruders but welcome them as friends!" Some Christians have asked, "Is James really serious? Surely the time to rejoice is when problems are on the way out, not when they're on the way in!" But no – when problems crowd into your life treat them as you would a long-lost friend – rejoice! James has a good rationale for making this statement: "Realise that they [trials] come to test your faith, and to produce in you the quality of endurance" (J. B. Phillips).

Our attitude in coping with opposition is of crucial importance. If we have the right attitude we can, as Paul put it, "turn evil to good". Opposition, envy and slander can all serve to make us draw on the character of Christ, and as a result we will become more like Him.

In all the centres of revival which I visit I am finding that trials and opposition are producing strong, tall, victorious, brave, daring and bold Christians. As General de Gaulle said, "Difficulties and hardships are good for men, for out of them we find ourselves."

When the Christian Church was suffering severe persecution under the Emperor Nero, the apostle Peter wrote to the Christians scattered among the provinces to encourage them. How did he do this? Did he tell them that things used to be much better back in the old days when Jesus Himself was in the flesh? Did he remind them that the Lord had walked on water and had healed sick people everywhere He went? Did Peter say, "You should have seen it!" No – he lifted his pen and wrote these fabulous words: "Though you have not seen him, you love him; and even though you do not see him now, you believe in him and are filled with an inexpressible and glorious joy, for you are receiving the goal of your faith, the salvation of your souls" (1 Peter 1:8-9).

Faith under opposition and persecution has an amazing vigour, a radical independence of all circumstances and a power to defy attempts to extinguish it. Under trial faith has a bouyancy, a heavenward ardour, a love, a depth and a height which it never achieves when things are easy.

Let us not be afraid of opposition. Samuel Rutherford said, "Let us turn our faces to the wind, brethren. Let us be prepared to face the storm for Jesus' sake." Jesus said, "Blessed are those who are persecuted for righteousness" (Matthew 5:10).

We must overcome opposition with love. Someone may be opposing you, but with Christ's love you can try to make a friend of them. A gift or a visit or a letter of appreciation (even if there isn't much to appreciate about the person!) can work wonders. Even the most difficult people have some good points which you can see if you look hard.

We must defeat our human enemies by loving them. But against the devil there can be only one strategy – *fight, fight, fight!* Make up your mind to fight him. "Be self-controlled and alert. Your enemy the devil prowls around like a roaring lion looking for someone to devour. Resist him, standing firm in the faith" (1 Peter 5:8-9). As you get out of bed each morning you need to remember that you are in a war. Heed the apostle Peter's warning, for Satan is determined to fulfil the sole purpose of his existence: to steal, kill and destroy. He has made his stand, and you must make yours. Be resolved in the core of your being that you are not going to be subject to the demonic spirits of this world and that you are going to fight them!

CHAPTER 18

Can a Revival Be Lost?

When our hopes break, let our patience hold.

(Dr T. Fuller)

Is it possible to lose a revival? This is a question which people often ask me, and I have to answer that history shows that a revival can indeed be lost. For example, the Lollard revival in the fourteenth century lasted only five to ten years; the Quaker renewal led by George Fox lasted not more than ten years; the Hebridean Revival lasted for only one year, while the Welsh Revival lasted for just nine months (although its wider influence went on until the late 1940s). Some revivals have lasted longer: the Wesleyan revival went on for 130 years, and the Salvation Army movement remained powerful for about 50 years. All these revivals were mighty for a time, but in the end they all lost their power.

What are the factors which curtail revivals? If we know what they are we may be able to prevent them from smothering the fire of the revival which is starting to burn in the UK today. There are three principal factors, and I see them rearing their ugly heads already.

The first one is *denominationalism.* The revial is transcending denominational barriers, but still people are putting their allegiance to their particular church body before their loyalty to the Kingdom. To some ministers and laypeople their church system is more important than God's blessing. Already people are putting up the denominational shutters. They are unwilling to abandon some of their traditions and to move with more liberty. This is tragic, because they will miss God's blessing.

Another possible probelm is *doctrinal disagreement*. The biggest theological split used to be the one between Calvinists and Arminians, but that is less in evidence now. Today the divisions are over the question of authority. The Restoration Movement's emphasis on "shepherding" has been highly controversial. Also, some churches are showing an unwillingness to cooperate with other churches which are not part of their particular authority structure. This sort of thing is dangerous and Spirit-quenching.

A third problem we have to watch out for is the question of *money*. When Christians get committed to revival and large numbers of people get converted the incomes of churches inevitably increase dramatically. Here there is scope for the love of money to get in and wreck God's work.

The course of the Welsh Revival has been outlined thus: "God began to work, and then the devil began to work in opposition, and then God began to work all the harder. And then man began to work, and the revival came to an end." It is essential in times of revival that a careful watch should be kept so that nothing which is not of the Spirit will be able to gain a foothold.

The revival has begun! Let's make sure that it doesn't die in its infancy or become a localized, isolated phenomenon affecting only certain parts of the country. May God speak to the whole land. Let every hamlet, village, town, suburb, city and metropolis be shaken to its roots by the good news that Jesus saves! Let people of every race, colour, religion, background and culture be moved by the heavenly message!